How to Flunk Out of College

of College

101 Surefire Strategies That Guarantee Failure

Fourth Edition

Cari B. Cannon, Ph.D.
Santiago Canyon College

ocn 924636779

Kendall Hunt
publishing company

Cover art drawn by Ryan Winn and colored by Bradley Johnson.

Kendall Hunt
publishing company

www.kendallhunt.com
Send all inquiries to:
4050 Westmark Drive
Dubuque, IA 52004-1840

Copyright © 2005, 2006, 2009, 2015 by Kendall Hunt Publishing Company

ISBN 978-1-4652-7647-6

Printed in the United States of America

CONTENTS

Chapter 3: Studying, Quizzes, and Exams   35

Chapter 4: Basic Skills and Assignments   59

Chapter 5: Time Management   75

Chapter 6: Grades 95

Chapter 7: Faculty 111

Chapter 8: Educational and Career Planning 129

Chapter 9: Personal and College Resources 145

Chapter 10: Apply It 161

Index 169

AUTHOR'S NOTES

All student names and other critical details in my vignettes have been altered to protect the innocent (and not so innocent).

I thank my husband and best friend, Dr. Robert Bramucci, for his assistance in writing this book.

INTRODUCTION

Like many students, I hated high school. I resented being told what to do by my teachers, I was bored in classes, and there were so many more fun things I could be doing. So I did anything *but* study, and by my senior year, I had a 2.5 GPA. Good enough to graduate but not good enough to get into a top university.

At the time, I wasn't even sure I wanted to attend a university. As much as I hated high school, why would I want to sign up for four more years of torture? During the summer between high school and college I did some soul-searching to try and discover what I wanted to do with my life, and I came to a startling realization: I *needed* college, not only to get a high-paying and rewarding job, but because I somehow understood that I would always have regrets if I didn't go. I already regretted being a bright student who got lousy grades in high school, and I regretted looking back on high school and feeling like a failure.

Since my grades weren't good enough for a top university, I registered at a community college. But this time I went to school with a goal: I was going to get straight As—whether I liked college or not, whether my teachers were good or bad, and whether my classes were boring or exciting. For the first time in my life, I took responsibility for myself and for my future.

I studied hard for my community college classes and ended with enough units to transfer to a major university. However, I didn't just pass my classes, I achieved a 3.96 GPA. This was important because I could look back on my first two years of college with pride and satisfaction. Looking ahead, I was nervous about going to what I thought of as "a real school" where the stakes were higher and competition was fierce. However, I discovered that my fear was unwarranted: I now believe if you learn good study habits, they'll transfer with you and you'll do just fine.

I left the big university with a bachelor's degree and a full scholarship to a doctoral program. The rest, as they say, is history. I have now been a community college professor for over a decade.

Although the majority of college students in America get their *start* at a community college, the reality is that less than a third of community college students complete a degree or transfer to a 4-year college! And, although many more Americans begin college, nationwide only about fifteen percent of them have a college degree. Why do so many fail? I'm sure these students, like me, enter college with plans and dreams. However, most students sabotage their own success because they fail to realize the most important fact about college:

The stakes have been raised

That is, college isn't high school, and by moving from high school to college, you're entering a different arena with different standards and competition. This is obvious in other areas, for instance, most people recognize that the star of a high school football team will likely not be a standout on his college team, or that the college star may never make the pros. Seemingly, however, students are not able to recognize this fact in relation to college. When they step onto the college campus, most students fail to realize that new strategies and behaviors are necessary; instead, they use strategies that worked in high school—and *they fail*. And unfortunately, the same strategies that lead to failure in college will likely lead to failures in career and in life.

This book will a) describe 101 ways to sabotage your education so *you* can be one of the many Americans without a college degree, and b) will include real-world examples of self-defeating student behaviors that I have encountered in my teaching career. You might recognize your own behaviors and wonder why you never saw these as detriments to your success. The book will explain what you are doing wrong and give suggestions to help you succeed. Along the way, you may discover that this book isn't really a guide to failure, it's a guide to success—it's just more fun than other college success books!

CHAPTER 1

Self-Perceptions

Imagine what would happen if you stood in the center of campus and told passers-by that you planned to kill your anthropology teacher? If you told enough people, might at least one person take you seriously enough to call the police? You bet!

What if, instead, you sat alone in the center of campus and just *thought* about killing your anthropology teacher? Will anyone call the police? No! That's because *there is no such thing as thought police.* If you don't share your thoughts with others, then no one will try to stop you.

The point is that while maladaptive *actions* tend to draw punitive consequences aimed at preventing such actions in the future, maladaptive *thoughts* usually go unchecked; therefore, they can persist for decades and lead to tremendous personal problems. Many students develop maladaptive, irrational self-statements such as:

- "I can't stand this class"
- "This should be easier"
- "I should've done better"
- "I'll never understand math"
- "I'm a failure"

Such beliefs become maladaptive when they interfere with your ability to succeed.

In this chapter, you'll learn to embrace and use irrational thinking to interfere with your chances at educational success.

1 Use Negative Self-Talk

One semester, I was teaching a research methods course. This course is a big deal for psychology majors because at many universities, if you get less than a B in the class you don't get to continue in the psychology program.

Paula approached me during office hours and said, "I'm really upset because I got an F on my first paper and this is a very important class for me—I can't continue without it. I'm afraid I'll never understand how to write like a scientist. It's just so different from any writing I've ever done and I'm rethinking my major."

I said, "You're right on both counts: this *is* an important class for psychology majors, and learning to write like a scientist *is* challenging. However, your decision about your entire career shouldn't hang on the first scientific paper you've ever written! I'm certain your writing will improve over the semester, and I'll bet that your fourth and final paper will be both easier to write and better written. Why don't you wait until the end of the semester to decide the fate of your major?"

Paula was skeptical, and continued to argue with me about her abilities.

I finally asked her, "I'm just curious, have you ever tried kickboxing?"

She was a little surprised by the turn in the conversation.

"No, but it looks really hard. Have you tried it, Dr. Cannon?"

"Well, about three years ago I went to my first kickboxing class but it was really embarrassing!"

"Was it really hard?"

"It wasn't so much that it was hard, it was just the movements seemed so awkward to me: my punches were pathetic and my back kicks looked like a dog trying to water a fire hydrant."

Paula laughed; I knew she was visualizing her professor making a complete fool of herself.

"I was actually stupid enough to stand at the front of the room, so everyone behind me, who had been regulars to the class for a while, snickered."

"How embarrassing! Did you ever go back?"

"I've been kickboxing ever since."

"No way! Really? Why did you keep going if you were that bad and everyone laughed at you?"

"Honestly, I remember telling myself that I should just go back to the dance-style aerobics that I had been doing for two years because I was already good at it. But then I reminded myself that the reason I took the kickboxing class in the first place was to recharge workouts that had become boring and predictable. I even told myself, 'It's good that I suck at this—it gives me a goal, something to improve on.' Besides, your body doesn't keep improving unless you keep challenging it. So I stuck with the class."

Paula was now suspicious of my motives in telling the story.

"So did you get better at it?"

"I'll put it to you this way: I've had two people independently ask me if I used to be a professional dancer because my kicks are so high."

"Seriously?"

"Yep, and now it's my favorite class at the gym! It reminds me that in the long run, being initially bad at something can be a good thing. Just think how you'd feel if you wrote a really great paper later this semester."

During finals week, Paula came back to my office to say that she is "starting to get the writing thing" and that the class has turned out to be one of her favorites. She believes she will continue to get better as she moves into her upper division course work and feels much more adequately prepared.

She went on to earn a B in the course.

Overemphasizing the negative aspects of a situation and ignoring the positive aspects is a *perceptual error*. As an example, if you received four As and one D this semester, what would you focus on? If you're like most people, you dwell on the single D. And although this is tempting to do, it's still, objectively speaking, irrational! It makes more sense to spend four times as much time praising yourself for the four As!

My point is that sure you should spend some time thinking about the D and what led you to earn such a low mark, however, don't forget to celebrate your successes. If you do, you'll keep your less-than-stellar performances in perspective.

We all have strengths and weaknesses. For example, some students excel at writing but struggle with math, while others intuitively grasp complex mathematical concepts yet have difficulty explaining themselves in writing. Dwelling on your weaknesses to the exclusion of your strengths is irrational. It not only harms your self-esteem, it prevents you from taking corrective action. Students who label themselves with terms such as "deficient," "dumb," or "worthless" rarely stop at merely using such labels—they begin to *dwell* on them, *internalize* them.

If you believe a failing is an irreparable condition, you're less likely to spend time on efforts (such as studying or getting tutoring) designed to overcome those weaknesses.

2 Believe You're a National Idol

One of my favorite TV shows was a widely viewed singing contest—you know the one—where you get to see all the people that didn't make it past the first audition. Like most people, I enjoyed the show for the same reason that people slow to stare at car wrecks: morbid fascination.

How can someone sing like a horse with its testicles caught in a vise yet still think they deserve to be a worldwide pop star? Who told them they were good? Family? Friends?

When the judges tell them differently, they're flabbergasted. Some even berate the judges by saying—"you just don't know *real talent!*" Is there really that much delusion in the world? Apparently, for I encounter hundreds of students every year who have similar delusions about their schoolwork.

Maria approached me after the third exam—the last day to withdraw a class loomed ahead—and she said, "I think I'm going to have to drop this class because I'm getting an F, and that won't look good when I apply to medical school."

"Medical school?" I asked, thinking she looked a bit young, but maybe she was a university student who was "slumming" at the community college for a class or two.

"Yeah, when I finish here I want to go to medical school."

"When you finish here?"

She said, "Oh, well I'm just a sophomore now, but eventually I'm going to medical school. This is my hardest class and I don't want to get an 'F' in it. If I drop this class, then I can pull up my grades in my other classes."

Huh? She's getting bad grades in her other classes, too?

It turns out she is getting a C in her remedial English class, and a D in a pre-college math course. This is really lousy work for a college student.

Well, just like the judges on the singing contest, I'm sorry but I have to be brutally frank—*college is not the place to tell students they can be anything they set their minds to be.* Don't get me wrong: when a child is ten, you cheer them on when they say they plan to be a movie star, the president of the United States, a doctor, or a Nobel-prize-winning scientist (or all of those simultaneously). But by college, it's *reality* time. It's notoriously difficult to get into medical school, so if you aren't acing your college classes, the odds are you aren't going to medical school.

However, Maria thinks if she wants it, she can have it, because hasn't this always been the case? Hasn't daddy always bought her whatever she wanted? New shoes? ("Sure, cupcake.") New car? ("Of course, snuggums.") New boobs? ("Whatever makes you happy, pumpkin.") But unless the medical school has daddy's name on it, he can't buy her way in. In a way, believing you're a national idol is the opposite of using negative self-statements; it's the belief that the rules that apply to other people don't apply to you because you're somehow special or entitled.

I actually have to confess to falling victim to this sort of thinking myself. When I was nineteen and a college sophomore, I drove around in my snappy sports car and laughed at people driving junky cars. "What a loser!" I'd say. What I didn't realize at the time was that the only difference between the guy with the ugly car and me was that my generous parents bought my car—I hadn't earned it myself.

In fact, without my daddy's credit cards, what was I? I didn't have the courage to even ask myself that question. I truly believed that I deserved whatever I wanted because I had quite simply always gotten whatever I wanted if I begged or whined enough for it.

The arrogance of my teen years has been replaced by the quieter confidence that comes from years of hard work and struggle. Don't get me wrong—I still drive a sexy sports car—but it's one that I earned by working hard and becoming successful and the car I earned myself is more personally gratifying than any car daddy bought for me. I now have more respect for a guy who works two jobs to get an old clunker than for a spoiled rich kid who gets a hot-looking car for free.

In the real world, away from the generosity of parents, nothing is free.

Students who believe they are national idols think nothing of asking professors for favors such as:

- Forgiving them for missing class to go on a family vacation
- Allowing them to clean out their teacher's filing cabinet for extra credit
- Making up a missed exam because they wanted to go to a concert for which it was hard to get tickets

For those students, it doesn't seem like a big deal to insist that they receive the rewards that everyone else had to work for. To them, I say, "Welcome to the real world."

3 Make Misattributions

Misattributions involve failing to accurately credit the causes of your behavior. Often, this means failing to accept responsibility for your own behavior and placing the blame on someone else.

This past summer session, my *Introduction to Psychology* class scored an average 62% on the midterm. Debbie, a rather bold student, asked, "What are you going to do now that we did so badly?"

"What do you mean what am *I* going to do?"

"Everyone did so badly, so aren't you going to do something about it?"

"No," and addressing the entire class, "if you aren't happy with your performance in this class who has to do something?"

"We do?" From a tentative voice in the far back corner.

The grade-grubbing student persisted, "I mean, are you going to give us some extra credit to help us raise our grades?"

"No."

She pushed some more. "If we do better on the final, will you overlook our earlier grade?"

"No!"

If you're thinking (as a few students in that class must have) that I'm a bitch, then I can live with that because I know that in the long run a student's immediate opinion of me matters less than her long-term opinion of me. Honestly, which teachers do you recall most fondly—-those who let you skate by with little effort, or those that made you work hard and learn something in return? I've had a number of students come back to visit after they've transferred to a big university. They almost always thank me for teaching in a way that prepared them for the U.

I *have* actually heard of teachers saying "Since you all did poorly, I'm going to make all of you retake the test for a chance at a better grade." This sort of practice leads students to believe that there will always be a second (and third, and fourth) chance. Such attitudes breed incompetence.

Let me give you a real-world example:

A woman who had surgery started having unusual pains. An X-ray indicated that the surgeon had accidentally sewn a pair of forceps inside her body! She was lucky—a second surgery removed the forceps and repaired the damage. I'm guessing the surgeon had teachers who let him or her have second, third, and fourth chances. Students might as well learn as early as possible that in the real world, the consequences of not doing something right the first time can be devastating. If you fall behind in your studies, it's important to see your instructor as soon as possible; however, what you say in that meeting can make or break your chances of receiving help.

Here are a few strategies that may hurt your chances of getting help:

Blame the Teacher

Tell the teacher that they didn't properly explain the material, or they didn't give clear enough information for you to prepare for the exam (e.g., "You never told us it was going to be an essay exam!") and so forth.

Blame Others

Who can you blame? Nearly anyone! Parents, other teachers, spouses, children, curve-setters—even the family dog—have been blamed for failing grades. In psychological jargon we call blaming others having an "external locus of control." Research shows that people with an external locus of control do more poorly in school than those with an "internal locus of control," who tend to believe that they can influence events by their actions such as studying hard to earn good grades.

Blame Bad Luck or Misfortune

Sooner or later every student has to deal with personal crises that arise during the semester. If you fall behind in your work, then such delays can be catastrophic to your grades. However, if you keep up with the work, you can usually accommodate sudden problems without devastating your studies.

One way to earn the respect of your teacher is to own up to your mistakes. Admit that you allowed yourself to get behind or miss a few too many classes, but emphasize that you're ready to improve. This is a great way to help you elicit the support of your professor, assuming it happens early enough in the semester to make a difference.

4 Compare Yourself to Others

In every class there is at least one student who excels when all others fail. You usually call them a curve-setter, brown-noser, or nerd.

I took a history course in college and *I* was the nerd. In the class, we had the opportunity to choose ahead of time whether we wanted to take a multiple-choice or an essay exam. Whereas every other student in the class chose the multiple-guess variety, I chose the essay exam. I had good reasons for choosing to write an essay: I like writing and I prefer to study general concepts and themes rather than nitpicky details.

I was the only student who earned an A on the first history exam. My fellow students concluded that the key to success was to choose the essay test from now on.

Fast forward to the second test, where a large number of students including myself picked the essay form. Again, I was the only student who got an A. My peers mistakenly believed that my As were somehow the result of good fortune. Wrong! It's simple. I studied, they didn't.

It doesn't make sense to envy those who succeed. Students who succeed aren't getting good grades because they're cute or because they've been washing the teacher's car. They almost always succeed by dint of hard work. They've *earned* their success. In fact, I got the sense the teacher of that history class didn't like me very much. I got an A in spite of our failure to "click."

Getting good grades becomes easier and less time-consuming with practice. Someone who is "acing" a class that you're struggling with most likely has more experience than you. Take for instance, the upper division psychobiology course I took in my junior year of college. I felt bogged down by the extraordinary number of terms. (Gosh, how many parts are *in* the brain?) The concepts seemed complex and tedious. I struggled to earn a B in the class.

Other students seemed to be having a much easier time than me. I wondered if I was intellectually deficient in some way. Why do I get As in all my other classes, yet I'm having so much trouble in this one? Then I learned that most of the students in the course were pre-med majors who were "slumming" and taking an easy class that reviewed material from many of the courses they'd already taken in their first two years. Most of the other students had previously taken a lot more physiology courses than I had. And it's likely that I am the only graduate of that course who now teaches psychobiology!

5 Employ a Lot of "Yes, Buts" and "Shoulds"

The "yes, but" people of the world love to rationalize. They make statements like:

- *Yes,* I skipped a lot of the homework assignments, *but* my attendance was really good.
- *Yes,* I know I was late with this assignment, *but* I had to take my mom to the airport.
- *Yes,* I missed class, *but* it was only because I had to take care of my little brother.

The problem with "yes, buts" is they're just excuses. If you missed an important deadline in your profession you have to live with the consequences: lost accounts, lowered pay, and after a series of mistakes, termination of employment. If you miss a class session or fail to get a paper in on time, accept the consequences like an adult.

If you're sitting there thinking "yeah, yeah, yeah," then imagine this scenario: the teacher promises twenty extra credit points to everyone who turns in a book report. You turn in a book report but don't receive the twenty points. Your teacher says, "I was going to give you the extra credit, but___." Not so agreeable when you're on the receiving end, is it?

"Shoulds" waste valuable time living in a fantasy world instead of focusing on what needs to be done:

- The teacher *should* make these tests easier.
- We *shouldn't* be expected to do this much work in this class.
- I don't think we *should* have to read this many pages.

You need to recognize that "shoulds" merely reflect your personal preferences. You wish the tests were easier, or that you didn't have to do so much work or read that many pages. The reality is that the tests aren't getting any easier, you indeed have to do that much work, and you do have to read that many pages. Accept the reality and do the only thing you can do in the situation: Adjust your behavior to meet the expectations. Period.

6 Practice Personalization

Some students see themselves as the main focus of attention, and assume that whatever is of utmost importance to them is of equal importance to the teacher.

Danny stopped me in the hall after class and mentioned that she was disappointed in the 65% she received on her midterm.

"Can you please tell me which questions I got wrong?"

"Sure. Stop by during office hours and you can go over your exam."

"Can you please just tell me *now* which questions I missed?"

I think to myself, is she nuts? Should I say, "Oh sure, you missed questions 10, 12, 23, 46, 51, 55, 57, 63. . ." just to mess with her? Get real! I have about 200 students each semester. Unless you're spectacularly bright—making perfect scores—I usually have no idea what you're getting in the course, much less which questions you missed on a single exam.

Another student elevated personalization to a level just short of psychotic:

Blake came up after an exam and said, "Why did you write that test question about my dad?"

"What test question? Who is your dad? I don't even know your dad."

"There was a question about a guy named 'Dudley,' who had multiple personality disorder, on the test. My dad is named Dudley."

"It's just a coincidence, Blake."

"I don't think so. I want to know how you know my dad, and why did you write that question about him."

"You're starting to scare me..."

Remember, people have their own concerns: it's *not* all about *you!*

7 Be Unscientific

The trick to being unscientific is to consistently ignore objective facts in favor of guesswork or opinion.

Renee fell asleep in class one day. I paused in my lecture to ask her to leave, go home, and catch up on her sleep. She was back in class the next day. Again she slept.

During a break in the class I invited her into my office to find out what the heck was going on.

"I don't really need to listen in class because I can get everything I need to know by reading the textbook."

"Really? What did you get on the midterm?"

"Oh, I don't know," she said, "How do we find out our scores?"

I showed her where they were posted. She had gotten a 42%. My dog could stamp out a 42% correct if you painted a twister board with a, b, c, d answer choices and some peanut butter.

"Yeah, I think you're right—you got that 42% all on your own!"

Renee *felt* like she was doing just fine, but the *evidence* suggested otherwise.

It's fairly common for students to fail to appreciate the consequences of their actions even when the consequences for those actions have been clearly specified ahead of time. For example, some students miss an exam and just assume it will be okay to show up weeks later and request a makeup. This happens to me in spite of the fact that my syllabus clearly states that makeups in my class will only be given for extraordinary circumstances and only if I'm notified within twenty four hours of the missed exam. I make it easy: the rules are written down. No need to rely on your intuition or make guesses; just consult the syllabus where all course policies are spelled out.

Amy gets 42% correct by chance.

Belle gets 42% correct by chance.

ryanwinn.com

This didn't stop Allen from requesting a makeup three weeks after the exam. He didn't have a doctor's note, but he offered to show me the nipple that was deformed in a piercing accident. No thank you!

If you take the risk, and the consequences are worse than you thought, be prepared to take the fall.

8 Be Unprepared for Challenges to Your Thinking

Alexandra wasn't happy with me for discussing masturbation in my *Introduction to Psychology* course. She complained to the dean, "When I was growing up, I learned that masturbation is wrong. My parents think it's wrong. My religion says it's wrong. Dr. Cannon talked about it like it's okay to do it."

In high school, your teachers had to watch what they said much more closely because they were teaching children. This is not true for your college professors who are allowed (even encouraged) to broach topics that will be uncomfortable for some students. I was discussing masturbation during class in conjunction with a chapter on human sexuality in the textbook. In that context it was a perfectly acceptable topic. And all I said was, "Despite what was once believed, modern research shows that masturbation doesn't cause any harm." Now, I understand that it might be inappropriate if I asked students to share their own tips on the best way to masturbate, but dispelling misconceptions with research is something professors do.

In college, expect to have your preconceptions challenged by others. Plan to feel slightly uncomfortable when you encounter new ideas that contradict what you have been previously taught. You don't necessarily have to change your thinking, but you do need to question it. That's what college is all about.

9 Catastrophize

"Now that I got a C in psychology, I'm never going to get into the teaching credential program!" cried Naomi.

"Does it actually say on the list of program requirements that you must get a B or better in psychology to get in?"

"No, but it says I need to maintain a B average."

"I'm sure one C isn't going to make or break your chances of getting into the program. If you get mostly As and Bs then it should average out okay."

"I'm afraid they'll look at that C and not want to let me into the program. Then what will I do?"

"Naomi, you're blowing this way out of proportion."

"Well everyone knows you need mostly As to get into a program like this."

"I don't think one C will make a difference either way. If you had all Cs then you'd have a problem."

"I don't know."

"I do. I've sat on several graduate admissions committees. I remember admitting a guy who had a couple of Ds."

"Really?"

"Yeah, his grades picked up as he went through college, he had great letters of recommendation, and extensive research experience. The committee chalked up the Ds to immaturity."

"So you think I still have a chance?"

"Sure."

It's natural to be disappointed when you get a lower grade than you expected. However, you have to be able to keep things in perspective. One bad mark is not going to ruin your life. Admissions committees don't care what you got in a single class; it's your overall GPA they'll consider.

STRATEGIES FOR SUCCESSFUL STUDENTS

- Keep negative thoughts in check by forcing yourself to emphasize the positive aspects of situations
- Get reality checks on your thinking by sharing your thoughts with knowledgeable others
- Assume responsibility for yourself and your success
- Take a *Psychology of Adjustment* or *Stress Management* course
- If you need assistance, get the help of a cognitive-behavioral therapist
- Continuously develop and improve your critical thinking skills

EXERCISE 1.1 *Self-Perceptions about Grades*

This exercise is designed to make you think about your perceptions of yourself as a student. **Answer the questions honestly.**

Do you see yourself as an A, B, C, D, or F student? Explain.

If your actual grades don't reflect your self-perceptions (e.g., for instance, you see yourself as an A student but you received a D on an assignment) what would you conclude?

When you receive a good grade do you attribute the grade to:
1. Your own successful skills and abilities
2. A kind or easy teacher
3. Good luck or good fortune

When you receive a bad grade do you attribute the grade to:
1. Your own lack of skills or abilities
2. A difficult or incompetent teacher
3. Bad luck or misfortune

Wait—you're not finished. Now go back and reflect upon your answers.

EXERCISE 1.2 Irrational versus Rational Self-Statements

Decide whether each of the following statements is rational or irrational. If the statement is irrational, write a rational alternative.

1. I'll never be able to understand this material.

2. I can't stand to get anything less than an 'A'.

3. I may not always have enough time to study as much as I'd like, but I will study regularly.

4. I can't write the perfect paper, but I can write the best paper that I can given my current skills and abilities.

5. I've always hated exams and I'll always hate them.

6. I don't have time to study.

7. I'll be humiliated if I fail this course.

EXERCISE 1.3 Reflection

Please use the following space to reflect on what you've learned from this chapter, and how it can be applied to your life.

CHAPTER 2

Classes and Lectures

> *Indifference: It takes 43 muscles to frown and 17 to smile,*
> *but it doesn't take any to just sit there with a dumb look on your face.*
>
> —*www.despair.com*

Have you ever heard the expression, "be careful what you wish for?" When I was seventeen and just about to start college, everyone treated me like a child: my parents, my older sisters, and my older coworkers. When I went to the mall or a restaurant the service seemed slower when I went with a friend than with my parents. My main wish in life was that people would treat me like an adult.

When I started college, I was delighted to finally have my wish come true. Looking back, the things that made me feel like I was getting adult treatment seem strange to me now. Although I'd always been a nonsmoker, I remember being amazed to see that other students were smoking on campus in plain sight. It surprised me because in high school, students hid behind buildings to smoke and they'd have gotten in big trouble had they been caught. I also observed students on the college campus sitting outside when they were supposed to be in class. I wondered, why there were no "hall passes" for those out loitering.

I guess I thought it was cool that college students didn't have to hide the behaviors that they once had to hide from high school teachers—they could be straightforward about the choices they were making in life. The assumption was that we were all adults capable of making our own decisions, good or bad.

But along with adult freedom comes responsibility, and responsibility means that if you make bad choices you have to live with the consequences. If you smoke long enough, you will likely get lung cancer or other smoking-related diseases; if you provide poor service for a client, then you may get sued; if you tell off your boss, you may be fired; or if you don't show up for class, you may fail.

As an adult you can't have it both ways, meaning you can't screw up and then demand to be cancer-free, keep your job, avoid a lawsuit, or pass the class. You have to own up to the consequences of your decisions.

In college, you will be treated as an adult and no one will actively stop you from making bad decisions. This chapter describes bad decisions students make in the classroom and the consequences they'll have to live with.

10 Blow It On the First Day of Class

It never fails: a student always shows up late on the first day, strolls across the front of the room, interrupts the teacher, and demands to be admitted to the class even though they aren't officially enrolled or wait-listed. Sylvia did a fine job of this when she entered my class a half-hour late, interrupted me, and asked if I was the T.A.

"Where is the professor?" she demanded.

"*I'm* the professor."

"YOU? Uh, I need to add this class."

"This class is full, and I have a wait-list, so you can wait around, but your chances of getting in are slim-to-none."

"I *have* to get into this class! It's the last one I need in order to get into the nursing program!"

What do you think? Would you let someone in, ahead of all the wait-listed students? Even though she was rude?

I guess she was one semester late.

I'm young for a college professor and look even younger, so I can understand that it's hard to believe I'm a professor. But if you have to make a mistake here, and you have a choice between mistaking the T.A. for the instructor or the instructor for the T.A. . . . do I really need to finish this sentence? Needless to say, interrupting class and insulting the teacher are not the best first-day strategies.

Of course, the best way to blow it on the first day of class is to miss class altogether. Some students decide that nothing important will happen on the first day. They expect to meet the teacher, receive a syllabus, and then leave early, so why waste a perfectly good morning?

But the first day of class is often critical. In fact, if you don't show up to one of my classes on the first day, I drop you immediately. I'm just following our college's policy, which, by the way, is stated at least five times in big, not so subtle boxes throughout our class schedule.

11 Arrive Late and Leave Early

Zeke arrived late every day, all semester long, strolling into class twenty, thirty, even sixty minutes late. He figured that if he showed up before the class ended and signed the role sheet, he'd get full credit for being in class.

When the semester was ending and students received their attendance and class participation scores, Zeke said, "You must have made a mistake on my score because I was here every day, I *never* missed a class, and I only received 50%."

"It wasn't a mistake. You were chronically late all semester, so I figured if you showed up for half the period, then technically you earned half credit."

He didn't get full credit because showing up for five minutes is not good enough to receive full attendance points. Every time he walked in late, he interrupted and distracted us.

Your professors expect you to arrive for class on time or even a few minutes early. Many students show up on time, but need to sneak out early for an appointment. Students that inform me ahead of time (assuming that this is done infrequently on their part) are usually excused. But try walking out without telling me and I might make a snide remark about your diarrhea problem to the rest of the class.

Other students don't attend class at all. Deidre missed the second exam of the semester. However, class policy was that I dropped the lowest exam score, so, she just had to make sure she did well on the other exams. On the final exam Deidre didn't show up until the last student was handing in his exam. She was over ninety minutes late!

"Oh, I'm so glad I made it!"

"You didn't make it—the exam is over."

"You *have* to let me take the exam, this is so important to me! It wasn't my fault I was late—there was an accident on the highway."

"I know the California freeways are unpredictable, but that's the same for everyone. Knowing that you already missed one test, you should've been here an hour early! Everyone else made it on time."

She actually (I kid you not) started screaming, crying, and pounding her fists on the wall. I've seen brats begging their moms for candy at the grocery store checkout lane who could take lessons from Deidre.

Like some other appointments in life, when classes are missed they cannot necessarily be made up. Sure, you can try to read the class material and figure it out on your own. However, the whole point of having a teacher is to expedite the learning process. A teacher can explain in a matter of minutes a concept that might take you hours to figure out on your own.

Ask any professor, and they'll tell you the same thing: the students with the best attendance consistently earn the best grades.

12 Ask, "Did I/Will I Miss Anything Important?"

Jake approached me after class one day, and asked, "I have to go to court next Thursday. Are we doing anything important in class that day?"

This question always raises my hackles. I asked, "Since I believe that *everything* I lecture on is important, what do you mean exactly?"

"Like, will there be any handouts or anything?"

I reminded him that handouts are always posted on the course Web site and asked him, "anything else you'd consider important?"

"I guess not."

"It's a shame though, that you won't be here."

"Why?"

"I've hired strippers to come to class and give free massages to everyone."

Okay, so maybe I didn't say that, but what's up with the "doing anything important" question? If you have to miss class, don't add insult to injury by asking your teacher this most dreaded of questions. The implication to the teacher is that the time she spent slaving over the lesson plans was worthless and that she's nothing but a glorified babysitter. Funny how a professor might take issue with that.

13 Assume It's Your Professor's Job to Go Over the Stuff You Missed

Suppose you had a fever of 103 degrees and understandably couldn't make it to class one day last week. Guess who's responsible for the missed material?

You.

The teacher already presented the material to the class and you missed it. With hundreds of students, he or she simply doesn't have the time to present it individually to each student who misses class. You wouldn't arrive at a movie theater late and demand that the theater show you the parts you missed, would you?

Please don't ask for a special showing as Mindy did:

"I wasn't here last week, can you go over the stuff I missed?"

"The notes are on the course Web site."

"Yeah, but can you just highlight what you actually said in class?"

"No. I already did that. You missed it."

"Did we watch a video?"

"Yes, in fact, we watched several clips from a few videos. You can ask whoever you get notes from about those as well."

"Can I watch the video clips now?"

"No!"

"What am I supposed to do?"

"Next time, show up to class."

If you missed class, ask your classmates to copy their notes or photocopy their handouts.

14 Pack Up Early

It never fails—when fifteen minutes are left in class, a few students begin to make a show of closing their notebooks, shuffling papers, and packing up their materials. This behavior is contagious; once one or two students have started packing, then a wave of noisy paper shuffling ripples across the classroom.

When the wave starts, I sometimes think out loud, "Hmm, should I go onto the next concept or stop there and save it for next time?" The students perk up, thinking that class is going to end a few minutes early.

"No, I think I'll just squeeze this last one in."

Hah! I might even go *over* a couple minutes. Maybe this is childish and vindictive on my part, but I never said I was mature for my age.

The professor decides when class ends. Period. Even if you're suffering, pretend you're still into the class. Either way, you leave at the same time. And you might just fool yourself into liking the class (or your teacher into liking you).

Disengaging early sends a clear message to the professor that you're done listening and are no longer actively involved in the class. Like me, many professors perceive this behavior as rude.

Now imagine that it's the end of the semester, and you're one point away from the next letter grade. Will you make it? Will the teacher bump you up? I doubt it. Imagine if, instead, you're still actively listening at the end of every class session and you're one point away from the next highest grade. Could it help? Probably. To your teacher, you stand out as an active and considerate student. Whenever a student is one point away from a grade, I always weigh their attendance and participation in the decision to bump them up or leave their grade as it stands.

15 Take Useless Notes

It was the first day of class on my first day teaching at the community college level. A smiling and eager student named Daniel sat front and center in the class.

I smiled back and introduced myself to the class, "Hello, I'm Dr. Cannon, and welcome to *Introduction to Psychology*." I noticed that Daniel wrote in his notes, "The teacher's name is Dr. Cannon. She welcomes us to the class." I thought, "You've got to be kidding! Did he just write that down? Why? Why did he write that down?"

I continued, "Today we will be going over the syllabus and . . ." Wait, he's writing! What's wrong with him? Is he going to write down *everything* I say? It was unnerving.

I didn't say anything to Daniel because I figured it was better to write too much than too little. However, later that day I noticed something astonishing. Daniel often did not write down the most important facts. I would present a main point like, "John Watson is considered to be the father of modern behavorism," and he just sat there. Now I was intrigued. Just to see what would happen I said, "You need to write that down, Daniel." He just smiled at me. Amazing!

After encountering a number of Daniels who wrote down less-important information such as stories and side comments but failed to write down main points, I wanted to make sure the most important points were written down without fault. Therefore, I made my lecture notes available to my students on the course Web site. Many students have told me they wished all their professors did this, but until they do, you need to learn to take effective notes.

One day I sat in on another professor's class in order to do an evaluation of the instructor. Looking around the room, I noticed that virtually all of the students were dutifully copying notes off the white board as the instructor wrote down the information. Most of the students wrote at other times as well. Obviously, they were jotting down the examples or stories to help them remember the main concepts later.

There was one student who sat at the back of the room without a notepad or pen. He just sat there. And sat there. Never wrote down a thing.

What if we tested the students, say two days later, to see who remembered the most from that day? You may think that the students who wrote a lot down will remember the most and the student who wrote nothing will remember the least. In fact, assuming that no one has reviewed their notes, then every one of the students who attended the lecture that day will likely have forgotten most of the lecture. This isn't a big surprise, because research on memory has taught us that most of what we are going to forget about a lecture we forget within one hour after listening to it.

So why bother taking notes at all? One purpose of taking notes is to help you *reconstruct* your memory at *a later time*. Those who take good notes will be able to use their notes to activate *retrieval cues*. Retrieval cues are words that help you remember more complex concepts.

A second purpose to note taking is to keep you actively listening to the lecture. If you're listening carefully, thinking about what is being said, and making decisions about which points are most important and should be written down, then you will remember more.

But if you *want* to fail your class, leave your paper and pen at home.

16 Avoid Participating in Class Discussions

Night classes are almost always the most lively and fun classes to teach, and this class was no exception. We were all getting into the material and having a good time. Everyone, that is, except Lane. He sat at the back of my classroom and surfed the Internet during the entire period (four hours!).

I didn't want to interrupt the class, so I simply switched off his connection using the master switch at the instructor's station, making it impossible for him to continue surfing. A short while later, I noticed that he was somehow back online. Apparently during a break in the course he had gone up to the front of the room and turned his connection back on!

The problem wasn't just that Lane was doing another activity during class time, but he was mentally disengaged from the class. It was distracting. And my syllabus clearly stated that you must attend *and* participate in class.

Some students can get away with multitasking (e.g., working on the computer and participating in class discussions at the same time). Van was a multitasker. He took class notes on his laptop and (I'm not sure he knows that I know this) he also occasionally played a game or two on the laptop as well. However, Van was a straight A student who always contributed to class discussions, volunteered for demonstrations, and answered any questions I specifically directed at him. I could tolerate Van's addiction to his computer.

Lane was a different story. He was receiving a low D/high F in the class. He was getting nothing out of the class and the class was getting nothing out of him. Everyone would have been better served if he had just stayed home and surfed the Internet to his heart's content. When everyone else in class is actively involved, one sullen student can suck the life out of the rest of us.

Entire classes, like individual students, have personalities. Some classes are fun and outgoing and everyone participates. Other classes are quiet and dull. Because of the nature of the course, I can usually count on my *Psychology and Effective Behavior* class to be an energetic one. In the *Effective Behavior* course, students pick a self-modification goal (e.g., to lose weight) and work on it over the course of the semester. As all the students are striving to improve themselves, they get advice from (and offer encouragement to) their peers. Students verbalize their fears about their projects and share successes and failures with the class.

At the end of the semester, I've had many students cry because the class was ending. They had become close to their fellow students and had gotten used to their social support.

One semester in the *Effective Behavior* course, I had a disproportionate number of quiet students. They rarely shared personal examples or opened up even when pressed. I'd ask if anyone had an example to share and I'd get blank stares in return.

Individually, many of my favorite students from past semesters were in the class. Collectively, however, the class was disappointing because I expected to have live bodies show up for class, not cardboard dummies. At the end of that particular semester, the only tears shed were mine—tears of relief.

From a monetary standpoint, I didn't lose anything by having a mute class; I still got paid the same. The real losers were the students, who didn't get as much out of the class because they didn't put much into it. Their attendance was good, but they weren't intellectually present.

Woody Allen is frequently quoted for saying, "Eighty percent of success consists of just showing up." I've never believed this! In college, showing up is less than half the battle. It's important in many classes to be actively engaged: ask questions, volunteer for demonstrations, and answer questions directed at the class. You will get more out of the class if you come prepared and get intellectually involved in the course.

I've heard every excuse under the sun from students who sit like deadwood during the class including the following:

- Shyness
- The belief that it's always better to listen than to speak
- The fear that you haven't anything intelligent to contribute
- The assumption that it's the teacher's job to run the class.

These are all mere excuses. If you don't participate, your grade suffers. Also, if I don't get to know you at all, I won't be willing to help you in the future (e.g., writing recommendation letters).

17 Never Do Homework

In my *Introduction to Biological Psychology* course, the homework consists of coloring pictures of the nervous system in a coloring book. It provides an enjoyable way to learn the basics of neuroanatomy. On a certain level, this has to be the homework assignment of your dreams: it requires a minimum amount of thought (you need only make certain that you color each anatomical part and the corresponding key term the same color) and you get credit just for doing it.

Every semester there are at least a handful of students that are just "too cool" to color. The result? They miss enough points to lower their grades by one-half of a letter grade! A "noncoloring" mid-C student consequently ends up with a D. What makes matters worse is if they'd kept up with the homework, they may have earned a B.

Think of these homework assignments that are graded on a "credit/no-credit" basis as a gift from the professor. They exist so less-talented students can get credit just for doing the work (you don't even have to color in the lines!). For those students who work hard but don't necessarily do extremely well on exams, the coloring assignment is a godsend.

If you bomb exams *and* miss homework assignments, then you're committing academic suicide in a manner befitting a Darwin award (Darwin awards celebrate individuals who kill themselves doing incredibly stupid things, with the effect of removing themselves from the gene pool).

18 Ignore the Syllabus

In college, I spent summers working in retail to earn spending money, only to find myself being asked at least ten times per day "Where's the bathroom?" It becomes really tiresome to answer these sorts of questions over and over (if you've worked at a restaurant or mall then you know exactly what I mean).

Professors hate having to repeat themselves. This is one reason we write a lot of stuff down.

Take the class syllabus. The major purpose of the syllabus is that it enables the professor to avoid having to answer the same questions a hundred times. "How many points is the exam worth?" "How many points are on the exam?" "Dr. Cannon, how many points . . ." I think you get the point.

What this means is if you approach the instructor with a question such as "is it okay if I miss class next week?" and her policy about absences is clearly indicated in the syllabus, then you risk annoying the instructor. Instructors expect you to not only read the course syllabus, but to have a working knowledge of it. I know a few profs who have gotten so fed up with students who don't read the syllabus that they make test questions from it.

Another reason for reading the syllabus is that every professor is a sort of independent contractor, so policies can vary widely between instructors. Some instructors are lenient about absences or due dates, whereas others may reduce grades for missed classes and refuse to accept late papers. You can never assume that what worked for one professor will work on all others. Instead, you must carefully read each course syllabus to know what the expectations are of *this* professor in *this* course.

Even if you have taken the same professor for another class, he or she may have different policies across courses. I teach five completely different courses with different requirements and expectations in each; in some, for example, I weigh class participation more heavily than in others.

19 Sleep in Class

My first year as an assistant professor, I taught a class that started at eight in the morning. Julie sat in the front row and every day she had the same vacant stare. I became convinced that she was sleeping with her eyes open. My hypothesis was confirmed when one day, she started drooling!

I spoke with Julie after class and learned that she had a grueling work schedule. I sympathized, but suggested that she either cut back on her work schedule or make changes to her school schedule. Why? Because sleeping in class is a complete waste of time—hers, the other students, and mine. She wasn't learning anything, and it was distracting to the rest of us.

There's no point being in class if you aren't even going to be awake. Besides, it's rude. However, sleeping in class isn't the only rude behavior. Anything that causes a distraction for others is rude as well. Some other examples include:

- Reading the newspaper
- Doing your homework
- Talking to other students
- Answering your cell phone
- Surfing the internet
- Zoning out

I have one thing to say about all of these behaviors: don't do them during class.

20 Disappear Instead of Drop

This summer I received a phone call from Chip, who was about to graduate from a university and apply to a graduate program.

"I took your *Introduction to Psychology* course two years ago, but my schedule was really hectic and I had to drop it. I was only there for a couple of classes."

"Uh huh."

Chip continued, "Well I was wondering if you could change my grade from an F to a W?"

"This was two years ago? And you only attended a few classes? Chip, I honestly don't even remember you."

"I was afraid of that since I was only in class a few times, and at the time I didn't think it would be a problem, but now I don't want that F on my transcript."

"Well, I'm not going to change your grade two years after the fact when I don't even have a memory of what happened. Also, the statute of limitations on a *legitimate* grade change is one year."

"I know but I was expecting to get a W that semester."

"Then you should have dropped the course."

"I assumed that if I stopped coming, that you'd drop me."

"You assumed wrong."

If a course isn't working out for you for whatever reason, it's *your* responsibility to officially drop it. This usually involves filling out a form and turning in the form by the deadline.

At least two or three students every year call me to let me know that they received an F in my course even though they were certain they dropped it. What they mean is they stopped coming to class. Dropping it means turning in the appropriate paperwork before the deadline.

One student swore so adamantly that he turned in his drop form on time that our registrar combed through the hard copies of all the forms from that semester. She was unable to locate the purported form. The student could not produce a copy either; likely, he quit attending the class but never took the time to officially drop and just hoped that it would all work out. But he learned an important lesson: either you officially drop the course, or you get an F.

21 Assume You Can Add a Class Late

A few students try to add classes after the first day and even throughout the first two weeks of the semester when it's still "legal" to add (maybe they are bombing a math class and their friend tells them about a cool psych class they have). So they show up and beg to be admitted.

One student came to my class for the very first time during the fourth week of the semester—the day before the first exam—and asked if he could add the class. I was shocked.

"You want to add my class? The first exam is tomorrow. There is no way you could pass this class now."

"I'd like to try. My friend is in here, and he'll help me study."

"No one can pull off a passing grade in that amount of time. The exam is tomorrow!"

"I think I can do it."

"There is no way I'm going to add you to the class at this late a date. It just isn't fair to the students who were turned away on the first day when I had a long waitlist."

The student actually said, "You're a bitch!" and stormed out. Something tells me he was not the next Einstein.

Even when I have admitted students after a week or two, it almost never works out. The students who are desperate to add my class late cause me the most grief because they don't know the class policies, are unaware of the exam dates, and don't ask their friends for missed information. Maybe they expect me to furnish this information.

The students who are last to add the class are almost always the first to drop a few weeks later. In the trade, we call these students LIFOs: *Last In, First Out.*

22 Monopolize the Teacher's Attention

Norman was a world-class brownnoser. He asked literally dozens of questions and made as many comments in a single class period. No sooner was a statement out of my mouth when Norman's hand would fly up, "Is that like . . . ?" or "Why does . . . ?" or "That happened to me once when I . . ." Many of Norman's comments were only tangentially related to the topic being discussed; sometimes they were completely unrelated. Replying to Norman was a waste of energy. I knew he would immediately come up with another question, so I often simply ignored him.

However, it was obvious the rest of the class could not ignore Norman. When he walked into the classroom, there were snickers, eye rolls, and negative comments. A student sitting two seats behind Norman even coughed out a "stupid jerk" at one point when Norman said something. It became so problematic that I actually had to pull Norman aside one day after class and tell him I was setting a two question per day maximum for him. "So you'd better think about which questions are the most important, before you ask them."

Here is the moral to the story: you want to stand out as a thoughtful and engaged student without looking like a freak. How do you accomplish this? Ask a couple of highly relevant questions (or provide a few appropriate comments) and then shut up.

23 Allow Yourself to Get Distracted

Jeffrey was taking one of my summer classes, but he never seemed to be paying attention: either he was dozing, daydreaming, or doodling. His grades reflected his lack of attention: he was getting a D in my class and an F in the other class he was taking that summer (and summer school was supposed to be a time for him to catch up). Imagine my surprise the day Jeffrey came to me and said, "I have a difficult time paying attention in my classes."

"I'm glad you recognize that about yourself. That's probably the first step toward fixing the problem."

"That's what I wanted to talk to you about."

"Okay, that sounds like a good idea. What's up?"

"I was sort of wondering, since you're a behavior modifier, do you believe that punishment works?"

"If used correctly, it does."

"Would you shock me whenever I'm not paying attention?"

"WHAT?"

"I saw this shock collar at the pet store and I think it might work."

"Shock you! Are you joking?"

"I'm totally serious. I want to pay attention and get good grades and I just can't."

"Honestly, Jeffrey, I'd love to shock you but it wouldn't be ethical or legal!" (Damn ethics and the law—I really wanted to shock him!)

Assume for a minute that I could shock him, that still wouldn't completely solve the problem; Jeffrey needed to learn how to monitor his own attention level and adjust accordingly, not depend on someone else to do his monitoring for him.

Together Jeffrey and I worked out a plan to help keep him on task. He wrote a reminder to "stay focused" on a tent card and kept it on his desk, he wrote out a few questions ahead of class and listened for the answers; I promised to thank him occasionally when he was paying attention. He got his other teacher to do the same. As the semester progressed, Jeffrey did improve a bit—and I didn't go to jail—so everyone won.

24 Expect to Be Entertained

Martin's eyes had that glazed far away look in them when suddenly he heard me say, "penis," and his head shot straight up. As soon as he looked at me, I seemed to be discussing something else. The rest of the class was laughing. I had a straight face. Martin looked dumbfounded.

I set Martin up. The day before, I told the rest of his class, "You know that guy Martin who usually sits right there next to Amy?"

"Yeah," most of the students in class said.

"Well, when he is here, he is rarely paying attention, unless I'm telling a joke or saying something off the wall. So next time he is in class and not paying attention I'm going to suddenly say, 'penis,' and see if he looks up." Everyone in the class (who were evidently as immature as I am) thought that it would be hilarious.

"Hey, did I miss a good penis joke?"

Now I can't help but laugh.

Half the class is clutching their guts, but this time, Martin *is* the joke.

I remember my college professors as slightly stuffy, so if you have a silly teacher like me, count yourself lucky. Whatever the teacher's personality, it's your job to learn. If you get a bonus trip to an improv comedy show to boot, then be happy because those tickets are at least thirty dollars per person for a one-hour show (not counting dinner, drinks, and the cover charge).

STRATEGIES FOR SUCCESSFUL STUDENTS

- Arrive on time every time for your classes
- If you have to miss a class, take responsibility for missing the class and getting missed information from another student
- Stay engaged during the entire class period
- Develop and use good note-taking strategies
- Contribute actively to class discussions
- Complete all homework on time
- Become intimately familiar with the syllabus
- Pay attention in class
- If you cannot continue in a class, follow the official drop policy

EXERCISE 2.1 Syllabi

Read over the syllabi for up to 3 of your classes this semester and answer the following questions for each course.

What is the name of the course?

Course 1	Course 2	Course 3

What is the professor's name?

Course 1	Course 2	Course 3

When are the professor's office hours?

Course 1	Course 2	Course 3

Describe the absence policy.

Course 1	Course 2	Course 3

Describe the makeup exam policy.

Course 1	Course 2	Course 3

When are the exams?

Course 1	Course 2	Course 3

What types of exams are given?

Course 1	Course 2	Course 3

What are the other requirements (e.g., assignments) of the course?

Course 1	Course 2	Course 3

What is the grading scale?

Course 1	Course 2	Course 3

EXERCISE 2.2 Syllabus Analysis

Choose a syllabus from one of your courses. Based on the syllabus, determine what your instructor's policy would be for each of the following examples.

1. Tarzan get thorn in foot. Him no visit medicine man. Him ask to make up missed exam. What happen?

2. Nicky Martin, a wannabe rock star, is on a concert tour. He's missed five classes before he suddenly remembers that he never told his professor he was going to miss class. What has happened to him in class?

3. Giff Jordan's race car misses a pit stop and he runs out of gas on the way to his final exam. Can he make up the final?

4. Hetta Jetsetta schedules a ski vacation to Aspen months in advance (when rates are lower) only to find out that the flight conflicts with a an exam date in her class. What can she do?

5. Bolt Upright finds the perfect term paper on the Internet and decides to pass it off as his own. What'll happen to him if he gets caught?

6. Nicky the Greek bets that the first test will be easy so he doesn't study for it. He loses the bet and bombs the test. Should he drop the class?

EXERCISE 2.3 Reflection

Please use the following space to reflect on what you've learned from this chapter, and how it can be applied to your life.

CHAPTER 3

Studying, Quizzes, and Exams

> **Failure: when your best just isn't good enough**
>
> —*www.despair.com*

Outside of college, even the most menial jobs involve training; for instance, you may learn how to work the cash register, how to operate machinery, or where to stock merchandise. However, unlike those off-campus jobs, unless you take a course in college success, then you typically don't get training in functions critical to your job as a student—memory, study skills, and exam-taking skills. Since studying and exams are such a big part of student life, isn't it odd that you don't receive the necessary training to do this aspect of your job well?

If you've never been trained to study for exams, you will not do much better than I did when I started my first job. At sixteen, I began working as a bagger at a grocery store. There was a shortage of available workers and they needed someone immediately, so I never went through the "required" training course. I had no idea what I was doing—and I had never even grocery-shopped for myself before! Consequently, I made terrible mistakes: I put eggs on the bottom of bags and threw cans on top; I put cleaning chemicals in bags with raw meat; I overfilled bags, causing them to tear and spill their contents. Apparently my naïve goal, "get everything in a bag as quickly as possible," wasn't in sync with the customer's goal of getting everything safely and conveniently home. I wasn't being careless on purpose—I just didn't have the knowledge that I needed to do my job well.

As a result of my poor performance, I was yelled at, cussed out, and had to re-bag almost everything for angry (and rightly so) customers, at which point I actually demanded training! I even thought to myself, "how dare the manager set me up for this kind of failure! He made me look like an idiot."

I wanted to do well in my job, and I meant well, but I hadn't been prepared. If you were the customer with squashed eggs and cleanser-coated chicken, would you care that I meant well? Would you give me credit for *trying* to do a good job? No!

Like my first day at the grocery store, college students are expected to jump right in and start studying and taking exams even though they lack the training to do well. Freshman often lack skills that professors assume are just common sense—just as my grocery store customers assumed it was common sense to put fragile eggs in the top of the bag.

Harsh as it sounds, your college professor doesn't care how hard you *try*, he or she only cares how well you *perform*. In order to perform well, you need to be prepared. How well prepared do you feel when you take an exam? Are you filled with anxiety because you didn't study? Are you often surprised because you did more poorly than you expected to do?

This chapter will show you how the untrained student bombs tests.

25 Don't Do Invisible Homework

I've heard it dozens of times, most recently from Randy on the first day of class, "Dude, this class is going to be a cakewalk—there's no homework! Just a few tests— I can handle that."

Weeks pass. Randy has shown up to class (when he felt like it), and taken exams (which he bombed). At home he has done virtually no reading or studying except for a couple of hours the night before each exam. Randy is puzzled.

"I've been doing everything I'm supposed to do in this class and I'm still getting a lousy grade. How is that possible?"

"Randy, you haven't been doing everything. You haven't been doing your *homework.*"

"Homework? But, there isn't any homework."

"There's *always* homework. You should be doing it every single day of the week."

"What homework?"

"Reading your text, taking notes, reviewing your lecture notes, and practicing for exams."

"We don't get any credit for that stuff!"

"Yeah, you do."

"No, we don't."

"Yeah, you do. If you do all the work, your test scores improve."

"You never told us we had to do all that!"

"Not explicitly. But those sorts of study skills are expected when you take a college course."

"Somebody should have told me!"

The funny thing about college is, *most* of your homework is invisible: never assigned, never turned in, and never graded. Yet your professors expect that you do a great deal of invisible homework. This requires knowledge of good study skills (which you can get by taking a "how to succeed in college" course) and a bit of initiative on your part (to apply those skills without being explicitly directed to do so). If you can't function as a self-starter and come up with your own plan for doing homework that was never assigned, then college may not be for you. Isn't that a kicker?

26 Miss Quizzes and Tests

Kurt was retaking my *Online Introduction to Psychology* course during summer session after he had gotten a D in it last spring. In this course, students were required to complete quizzes on the course website. The quizzes were worth fifty points graded on a credit/no credit basis. All the students had to do was take all the quizzes, and regardless of their scores, they got the full fifty points (of course if they wanted to do well on exams, it made sense to aim for high scores on the quizzes, which have similar questions, but that's besides the point).

Kurt missed enough quizzes to knock his quiz grade down to a 41/50 and ended up with a total 204 out of 300 points or a 68%—earning himself a second D in the course. Had he finished the assigned quizzes and received the full 50 points for them he would have received a 213 out of 300, which averages out to a 71% or a C. Go figure!

By blowing off those weekly quizzes or pop quizzes, you lose points so gradually you hardly even feel it. However, all those little ten-point quizzes add up. If you missed all the weekly quizzes, you, like Kurt, would probably lower your grade by one full letter. Once in a while, a student in Kurt's position will try to beg for the nine points. I find this insulting. If you want those critical points, *do the work*. When all the points are in, and grades are assigned, it's too late to grovel. Groveling may work with parents, but it doesn't work with professors.

If failing a little bit at a time is too slow, you can do it in one swoop by missing a big exam. If you don't show up for major exams in my classes, then you'd better be comatose; otherwise, you will likely fail the class.

If you do miss an exam, don't just assume it can be made up. Look at your instructor's makeup exam policy in the course syllabus before you decide whether it's worth it to miss the exam. If he or she has a strict no makeup exam policy, you might want to grab your barf bag and head to class. Even if your instructor allows makeups, they may be more difficult than the original exam.

In an effort to be both fair to students and to avoid inconvenience on my part, I have experimented with different policies for missed exams over the years. I've tried:

- Dropping the lowest exam score
- Using all test scores, but allowing a makeup with a doctor's note or similar unavoidable emergency
- Allowing students to retake (or makeup) one exam in lieu of a final exam

For instance, one semester my policy was to drop the lowest exam score for everyone. If you missed an exam, it wasn't a big deal—I would just drop the one you got a zero on. If you took all the exams but did poorly on one, I'd throw out your score on the worst exam. If you aced all your exams, then you could skip the final exam (earning a zero on it) and I'd drop that score. Dropping the lowest exam seemed fair. It allowed every student one "break" and meant that all students received the same treatment.

After using this policy—one break per student—I discovered that if students are allowed one break, then they ask for two, which leaves me little incentive to offer the first break. For instance, someone might miss the first exam and then ask for a makeup exam. That is the equivalent of saying, "I know everyone else gets one break, but I should get *two.*"

Jeri tried for a second break.

"I was sick and didn't take the exam. Is there any way I can make it up?"

"Don't worry about it, that's exactly why I drop the lowest exam score. You just need to do well on the remaining three exams and the missed exam will have no effect on your grade whatsoever."

"But I'm worried that I might not do well on one of the exams that are left and then I'm screwed."

"In that case, you'd better hit the books, and don't stop studying until the semester is over!"

"It really isn't fair, because now everyone else gets to drop one of their exams and I don't because I didn't get to take one."

"Actually, that is perfectly fair. I excuse *one* exam for *everyone,* regardless of the reason. That way, you don't even have to tell me why you missed an exam, or explain to me why you bombed one. It's a 'get out of *one* exam free' card. No questions asked."

"I still think I should be able to take the exam."

Jeri just didn't get it at all (maybe a shock collar isn't such a bad idea after all!).

27 Don't Study for Tests; After All, You May Get Lucky

Many years ago as a graduate teaching assistant, I discovered something amazing: you can give college students the exam questions ahead of time and many will *still* not prepare for the exam!

I was the graduate teaching assistant (TA) for an upper division *Behavior Modification* course. The professor gave students a list of fill-in-the-blank and multiple-choice questions, from among which he would choose some to be placed on the midterm. He told the students to fill out this practice exam and bring their answers to the TA's (my) office to be checked over. All of the exam questions would come from the practice exam. The instructor told me to help anyone who shows up and even give out the correct answers.

Guess how many students visited me?

If you said *zero,* you're right.

I wondered: did getting the exam questions ahead of time give students a false sense of security? Were they just plain lazy? Or was it so just more fun to be surprised by the questions? Whatever, it makes no sense not to use the study resources that have been provided for you.

In my own classes, I offer a study guide, which lists the concepts that will be covered on the exam. In case you missed that last sentence, let me repeat it—my study guide *indicates what is going to be on the exam.*

When polled, at least 40% of the students in my courses indicated that they did not even use these study guides! Some had excuses at the ready: "I didn't realize that's what they were," "I couldn't get onto the course Web site to access them," and so on. Of the remaining students who used the study guides, it appears few used them well, if the class exam scores are any indication. What's happening here?

Take Ricky as an example. Ricky visited me during office hours to ask questions about his study guide. Since so few students take the time to do this, I tried to be as helpful as possible. There were several questions on the study guide that Ricky claimed he "couldn't find" in the textbook or lecture notes. He must not have looked very hard because I could go straight to these materials and point to the information in the textbook or lecture notes. Oops! The reason Ricky had trouble "finding" answers is he waited until the night or two before the exam and tried purposely hunting for the answers and ignoring everything else. This is backward. You're supposed to study first and then use the study guide to highlight items that you should emphasize for additional study.

For those questions on the study guide that Ricky did answer, many were incorrect or incomplete. For example, one study guide question asked, "How do nerve cells communicate?" Ricky wrote, "with chemicals called neurotransmitters." This is factually correct, however, this is only part of the story. My test bank has five different questions about neural communication. If I decide to put all five questions on the exam, Ricky has a shot at getting only one of those correct. And a 1/5 is a 20%, or a big, fat F.

If you want to do well on exams, then you need to do at least four things:

1. Study
2. Study enough
3. Study the right material
4. Study effectively (or use the right techniques)

28 Assume Reading and Remembering Are the Same Thing

When I lecture on human memory, I ask students to share their personal study tips. Most students indicate that they read their textbooks (hmm, a rather obvious tip). They also say that in order to remember important information, they reread it. On the surface, this seems to make sense: if you really need to remember something, the best way to remember it is to read it over and over again. However, if you believe that, you're wrong. You read text to *comprehend* it, but to *remember* the material other strategies work far better than rereading.

Reading and rereading your text is actually a fairly worthless strategy if you're attempting to remember the material! In fact, reading and rereading material is worse than worthless, because it creates a false sense of confidence: each time you reread a passage that you have read before, your previous exposure makes it seem increasingly familiar. This tricks you into believing that you will remember the information.

Professors purposely write their test questions with decoy answers that seem correct because they are familiar. If that seems like we are being purposefully deceptive, just remember, we've been playing this game a lot longer than you have. We know how to separate those students who truly understand the material from those who just memorized it.

Your fantasy test questions probably look like this example from *Introduction to Psychology:*

_____ was a Russian Physiologist who studied salivating dogs.

a) Mickey Mouse
b) Donald Duck
c) George Washington
d) Ivan Pavlov

The correct answer (d) jumps out at you as obvious, because:

● You may remember reading about Pavlov in your *Introduction to Psychology* textbook, so this answer is familiar to you. You get that "I recognize that one!" feeling.
● You're pretty sure the others haven't anything to do with psychology.
● Almost everyone knows the answer to this question even without taking psychology.

In actuality, your instructors are not going to ask questions that any bozo plucked off a random street corner could answer. It defeats the whole point of the exam: to make sure you learned what you were supposed to learn from attending the class and studying the current chapter(s).

An actual question might look more like the following:

_____ was a Russian Physiologist who studied salivating dogs.

a) Pavlov
b) Thorndike
c) Skinner
d) Watson

Uh, oh. Here the answer is less obvious because all of the people offered as answer choices were discussed in the chapter on learning, they all seem familiar, and you need to know the different contributions of each to pick out the correct response.

Unprepared students complain about these sorts of questions as being "trick questions." Nonsense! The question does exactly what it's intended to do—it screens out those students who actively and thoroughly learned the material from those with a passing familiarity.

The assumption that reading automatically leads to remembering has been refuted by decades of research on the cognitive psychology of human memory. Memory researchers have discovered that you must actively *think about* and *reflect on* what you're reading.

However, even thought and reflection aren't enough: to be able to retrieve the memory reliably, you must also practice retrieving the information. This is called *retrieval practice,* and it means preparing for exams by doing what you will be doing when you take an exam—answering questions.

Take a look at the preface to a few of your textbooks. I'll bet each of them recommends using some sort of letter/number strategy to study: PQ3R, SQ4R, PRTR, or something similar. What do all these techniques have in common? They demand that you ask and answer questions! So instead of reading, "Pavlov was a Russian physiologist who studied salivating dogs" over and over again, what do you do instead?

You ask yourself:

- "Who was Pavlov?"
- "What did Pavlov contribute to psychology?"
- "Where did Pavlov come from?"
- "What was the name of the guy who studied salivating dogs?"
- "What did the study of dogs do for psychology?"

And so on.

This technique works because you're practicing what you will be doing on the exam: answering questions. When you do this for all the material you're supposed to study and you can get the correct answers without looking at your notes, then you're good to go!

29 Blame Lack of Studying on Laziness

One day in my *Psychology and Effective Behavior* class I asked students if anyone thought their GPA was lower than it should be based on their abilities. Several hands went up. I asked Leann to explain.

"I know how to get good grades; I just don't because I'm too lazy to study."

"Well, I'm glad that you know what you *should* be doing. I just don't quite understand what it is that you *are* doing."

"I'm not doing anything. That's sort of my problem."

"You are always doing *something:* watching TV, eating, talking on the phone."

"Well, yeah, that's true."

"So can you tell me what you are doing when you should be studying?"

"I guess, if I thought about it."

The point that I was trying to steer Leann toward is: laziness isn't a *condition,* but a *behavior.* What's the difference? If you think it's a condition, then you aren't likely to do anything about it. You'll just shrug your shoulders and say "Hey, I can't help it, I'm lazy." But if you think of it as a behavior, then behaviors can be changed, influenced, even controlled.

How do you control behavior? The first step is to observe them. What are you doing when you should be studying? The next step is to make a plan so these temptations do not prevent you from doing what you should be doing. For instance, if you are always watching TV when you should be studying, then maybe a big sticky note on the TV screen reminding you to study might work. Or if you are always on the phone with your friend Susan, then ask Susan to remind you to study or refuse to talk to you when she knows you should be studying.

Of course, studying doesn't mean you have to give up the activities you like. Once you've studied, you can allow yourself a bit of TV or phone time as a reward.

But just in case you *are* truly lazy, I've seen (in one of those crazy gadget catalogs) a recliner with a built in toilet. Now that's LAZY!

30 Only Study Bold-Faced Words

Unlike high school, college is more about mastering complex concepts than memorizing and spitting back facts. However, the most frequently used study technique by college students is the good old "flash-card-word-definitions" method, with bold terms listed on one side and definitions on the other.

If you study vocabulary words this way, without linking them in any way to higher order concepts, then you may be in big trouble because the further you go in college the less likely you will be able to stop at just simply memorizing a few key terms. What are you missing when you focus solely on bold-faced words? You're ignoring interrelationships between concepts. "So what?" you ask. The big deal is this: you aren't taking advantage of how your memory system *actually works.* Most of your memories are not stored like those discrete, disconnected flash cards you've been using. And because you're using an "unnatural" way to memorize material, it becomes needlessly difficult.

To understand how your memory system *does* work, let's stop for a minute and think of all those old western shows on television where a cowboy rides into town, dismounts his horse, and heads into a saloon. What does he always do just before entering the saloon? He ties his horse to a hitching post. Why? Because he wants his horse to be there when he comes back for it!

Similar to the cowboy, you want your memory to be there when you come back for it—especially during an exam. How do you make sure the memory will be there when you need it? It, too, needs to be tied to a hitching post.

Your brain is full of memories that were *automatically* "hitched" to other memories. For instance, there is a library building at UCLA that is forever linked in my mind to the image of a girl with her skirt caught accidentally in her underpants. One day I was walking outside the library when I noticed to my horror that this girl's skirt was tucked into her panties. I quietly mentioned the problem to her and she ran off to fix herself, looking very embarrassed.

This was horrifying (OK, who am I kidding? It was hilarious!) Now, I didn't set out to purposely memorize "when you think of the library, think of the girl with her skirt caught in her panties," the connection happened naturally and effortlessly. But let's get back to the topic at hand: the hitching post.

The hitching post in this case, your memory system, is arranged in what is often called a *semantic network*. A semantic network is a set of concepts that are interrelated such that thinking of one concept will likely bring related ones to mind as well. Figure 3.1 displays a portion of my own semantic network, where concepts are depicted in bubbles called *nodes* and arrows link related concepts and allow activation to spread from node to node.

When I think of the concept "UCLA," assume I activate the "UCLA" node in my memory system. Picture it lighting up. Almost immediately, this activation spreads down the links to related concepts. For example, thinking of "UCLA," leads me to think about the "library." This makes me think of "woman with caught skirt," which leads me to think about "embarrassment" and so on.

The more closely two items are related in your mind, the more likely it is that thinking about one will lead to activation of the other. For instance, when I think about UCLA it's likely that in addition to unfortunate underwear episodes, this will lead me to think about what I spent a lot of time doing there: studying, researching with rats, and teaching children with autism.

More importantly, if I want to remember something about UCLA, and I'm having difficulty, I can use related information to help me activate what I'm looking for. For instance, about a year ago I visited UCLA (I had not been on the campus for about fourteen years) and was having trouble remembering which building contained the library. I remembered myself standing in front of the library, seeing the woman with her skirt caught, and thought to myself "oh, *now* I know where it is."

What happened here to help my recollection? At first, the image of how to get to the library was too vague for conscious recall—it wouldn't light up—however, as soon as I pictured myself as a witness to the woman's embarrassment, the activation of that concept spread additional activation to the related library concept and helped me to retrieve the memory.

What does all this have to do with studying? Have you ever been in the middle of an exam and hit a question where you felt the answer was on the tip of your tongue but you just couldn't bring it to mind? When that happens, the item is probably in your memory, but you just can't seem to trigger it. This is called a *retrieval failure*. It happens when there isn't enough activation to trigger the concept you want to retrieve. The concept is in there, but it lights up so faintly that it never enters consciousness. And when this happens, you're probably going to miss the question on the exam.

Back to the definitions. Say you've memorized a concept using the bold-word-flash-card technique, and it's floating around somewhere in your memory system. However, *you never tied this memory to a hitching post,* and now you're in the middle of the exam thinking "Where did the damn thing go?"

Are you surprised when this happens? How can you prevent it? Don't throw your flash cards out, just yet. Instead, grab them and arrange them into a sort of semantic network. Think about how the item on one card is related to all the others. Sort them. Organize them.

*For the diagrams in Figures 3.1 and 3.2, I used a terrific computer program called *Inspiration*. It allows you to make concept maps and include notes, pictures, and many other features into your diagram.

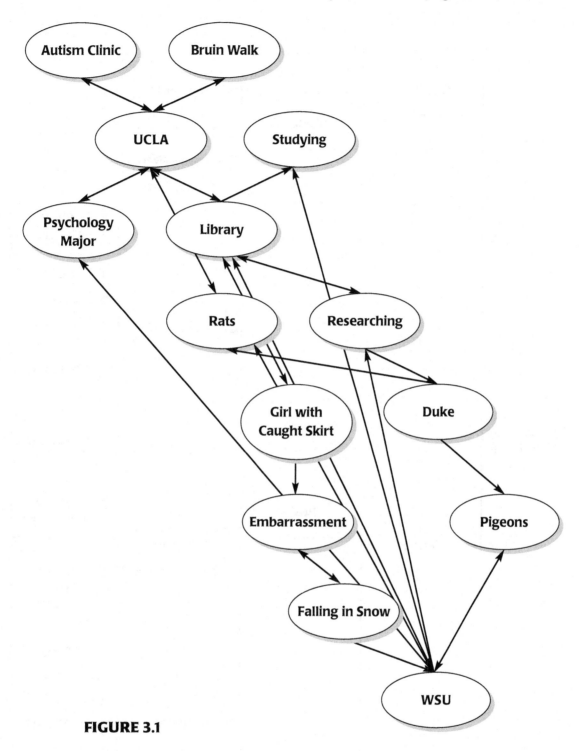

FIGURE 3.1

Figure 3.2 shows an example of how you might arrange your flashcards (although my example is computer-generated to make it easier for you to see)* in an *Anatomy and Physiology* class. You'd put the name of a structure on one side, and the definition on the other. Then you lay out the cards in a tree diagram shape, showing how all the information is related. For instance, from looking at the arrangement, it's clear that the hippocampus is a part of the forebrain, which is a part of the brain, which is a part of the central nervous system.

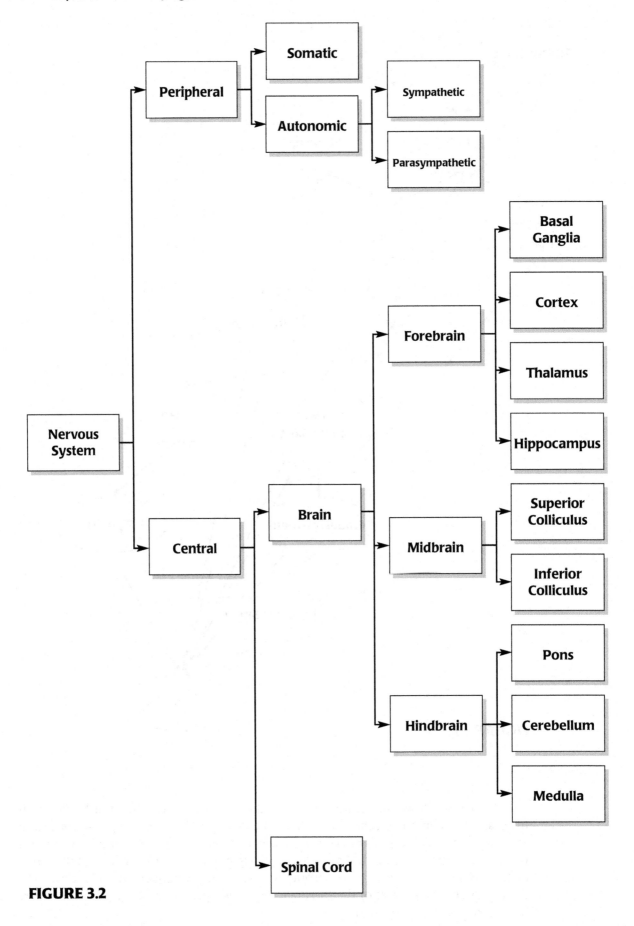

FIGURE 3.2

When you have all your cards set up this way, now you're ready to learn! What do you do with them? You need to be able to

1. Call out the information on side two while looking at side one (this is what you usually do).
2. Call out the information on side one while looking at side two (hopefully, you usually do this, too).
3. Arrange the cards into the organized pattern from memory.
4. Shuffle the cards and do it again.

Of course, you're welcome to skip the cards altogether and draw your diagram on a single piece of paper (or do as I did and use a computer).

31 Cram

My teacher's intuition suggests that most students wait until the night or two before an exam to begin studying. Could I be wrong?

To find out, I gave out an anonymous paper and pencil survey to my courses. One of the questions asked students whether they studied over several days or whether they crammed for the first exam. Sixty-five percent of students admitted they crammed.

If you cram, then it's because you're ignorant (and dare I say, a bit behind the times) of research in cognitive psychology that has been around since the early 1900s: on the comparison between the effects of distributed versus massed practice on memory.

Distributed practice means studying a little at a time, with rest periods (days) between study sessions. *Massed practice* means studying all at once (cramming). Distributed practice has been repeatedly shown to work better than massed practice for long term retention. So let's say a pair of identical twins, Jeff and John, were each willing to spend four hours studying for an exam as follows: Jeff used distributed practice and spent one hour Monday, one hour Tuesday, one hour Wednesday, and one hour Thursday studying (for a total of four hours studying for Friday's exam). John used massed practice (i.e., crammed) and spent four hours studying Thursday night.

Who is going to do better on the exam? To make it easier for you, let's make this a multiple-choice test:

(a) Jeff, because distributed practice is better than massed practice for long-term retention of information.
(b) John, because massed practice or cramming keeps information fresh in your mind.
(c) They will both do about the same because they both spent four hours studying.

If you've been paying attention so far, the correct answer is (a).

Let me summarize this chapter so far. To do well on exams you must

1. Use retrieval practice (practice answering or rehearsing questions for the test).
2. Make sure you're retrieving both key words and interconnections between concepts.
3. Distribute your studying over time (e.g., several days or preferably weeks).

Or in the words of cognitive psychologist Ulric Neisser:

You can get a good deal from rehearsal.
If it just has the proper dispersal.

You would be an ass
To do it en masse:
Your remembering would turn out much worsal.

32 Don't Learn or Use Any Memory Techniques

Buddy, an excellent student, was taking his second class with me. One day before class he stopped to talk to me.

"Dr. Cannon, what was the name of those memory techniques you taught us last semester?"

I laughed, "That's a little ironic, don't you think?"

"What is?"

"You forgot the name of the memory techniques. That's funny!" I'm not sure he got it.

Anyway, the name for the memory techniques is *mnemonics*. Mnemonics are tools that you can use as shortcuts to remember information that is difficult for you.

Perhaps you have used the mnemonic "Thirty days hath September . . ." to help you remember how many days are in a month? Or maybe your physiology professor used something similar to the following to help you remember the names and the order of the twelve cranial nerves:

On **O**ld **O**lympus' **T**owering **T**op **A** **F**inn **A**nd **G**erman **V**aults **A**nd **H**ops

where the first letter of each word stands for:

Olfactory, **O**ptic, **O**culomotor, **T**rochlear, **T**rigeminal, **A**bducens, **F**acial, **A**coustic, **G**lossopharyngeal, **V**agus, **A**ccessory, **H**ypoglossal

Many additional mnemonics exist, from peg word systems to the method of loci. You don't need to invent them yourself—just locate the ones that will work for you.

When should you look for a mnemonic? Anytime you're trying to memorize a list of items that is unfamiliar and difficult for you: all the former presidents of the United States in order, the articles in the Bill of Rights, a lengthy formula, and so on.

Where should you look? It would take too much time and space to go into detailed mnemonic systems here, so I refer you to a nice site on the Internet for further resources: http://www.mindtools.com/memory.html.

33 Avoid Using Study Materials

When I look at today's textbooks, I'm filled with envy. They come with a huge assortment of prepackaged supplements and study aids: a study guide, a CD-ROM with tutorials and practice quizzes, and sometimes a companion Web site with a host of study resources such as digital flash cards. Why the envy? When I went to college, all I got for my money was the textbook. I had to create or invent my own study materials.

The study resources that come with your textbooks are usually geared specifically to your textbook, and were written by the same people who wrote your textbook and the test bank from which your instructor selects exam questions.

If you ignore all of these resources, then you deserve to fail.

34 Ignore Test Anxiety

Early in my teaching career I encountered a student, Trina, who during the first exam of the semester was so wracked with test anxiety that she actually screamed out loud in the middle of the exam. Startled, the rest of us turned to look at her, but she was oblivious to anything except her own anxiety-filled world.

Every time Trina got to a question she wasn't certain about, vocalizations ensued. The situation was unusual because Trina was a straight A student. I stopped her after class and suggested she see the campus psychologist to discuss her test anxiety. Over the course of the semester, as she worked with the therapist, I could visibly see her anxiety diminish as she took Exams 2 through 4.

Allow me to correct a common misconception. Many students think of "test anxiety" as *any* form of anxiety during an exam. That's wrong. If you're taking a test and feeling anxious because you haven't studied, that's not test anxiety! It's a completely rational response (if you didn't study, you should be afraid, be very afraid!) That is, if you're underprepared for an exam, the resulting anxiety and poor performance is entirely predictable. Nor is test anxiety the normal amount of nervousness we all get when we're being evaluated. *Real* test anxiety is when you've studied hard and know the material, yet your anxiety reaches levels so high as to prevent you from demonstrating what you know.

The single best way to deal with the stress of exams is to be prepared for them. The sooner you prepare, the better. Your goal should be to be ready to take the exam at least one full day before the exam so that you could relax the day before. This may seem impossible, but it can be done and it works wonders on your anxiety levels.

Besides performing well on exams, you need to learn to relax for "real world" performances as well. It's a fact of life in many professions that you will have to perform well under pressure. Imagine if you were a professional athlete, an actor, a trial lawyer, or a surgeon; you'd need to perform well in spite of your nerves.

35 Don't Read Directions

On exam day, Maria handed in her exam and rushed out of the classroom. As she left, she wondered to herself why the exam only had forty-three questions; however, she just shrugged and didn't think about it again until she saw she had failed the test.

It turns out that she somehow "forgot" to complete the last page of her exam. When she discovered this, she demanded an opportunity to complete the exam.

"Sorry," I told her. "The directions on the cover page of the exam specifically stated 'Choose the best answer for each of the following 50 questions.'" Not only had she missed the last seven questions; she also failed to read the directions. Had she read them, she would have realized her mistake *before* the exam ended.

Maria's not alone in failing to read direction on exams. On one computer-graded "fill-in-the-bubble" exam, in spite of the directions indicating that students must use a No. 2 pencil, one student used a ball-point-pen, another used a marker, and a third used a highlighter. What the heck?

36 Say, "I Knew the Material, but the Questions Were Worded Funny"

Anytime I hear this phrase (and I must hear it at least five times for every exam I give), I shudder. Why? This is complete crap! If you knew the material, you'd do well on the exam. If you did poorly on the exam, then you didn't know the material.

To make understanding this concept easier, assume you memorized the following concept:

"The man kicked the cat."

Now you're taking the exam and you encounter a question in which the correct answer reads:

"The cat was kicked by the man."

"Oh my!" you think, "I don't recognize the right answer. I thought the answer was 'the man kicked the cat' and I don't see that choice here."

Seriously, if you can't pick out the correct answer, then either

1. You memorized information without comprehending it, or
2. Your brain cells are so disconnected that you'd need email to send messages from one cell to another.

You need to *overlearn* important material. This means, knowing definitions backward and forward, inside and out.

I have a few recommendations for anyone who thinks they failed because the test questions were worded funny:

1. Read for comprehension before sitting down to memorize information.
2. Read a second, and even a third textbook on the same subject when you study, so that you can be sure you're really learning and comprehending what you read and not just memorizing definitions word-for-word.
3. Ask someone who is not in the class, but who is familiar with the material, to quiz you.

37 Say, "But All My Finals Are on the Same Day!"

"Is there any way I can take the final on a different day?" asked Tommy.

"No. You have to take it at the scheduled time, otherwise I'd have to let everyone take the exam at their convenience."

"Yeah, but I have three finals that day. That's ridiculous."

"No, that's college."

If you have kept up with your work throughout the semester then it really shouldn't matter if all your finals are on the same day. If, however, you waited until the week before finals to begin studying a semester's worth of material, you're screwed.

You can avoid a big shock at semester's end by looking at your college's final exam schedule when you sign up for classes. Plan ahead or at least become aware of what you're getting yourself into. The final exam schedule isn't a mystery; it's probably published right there in the *Schedule of Classes* with all the other pertinent information for the current semester.

38 Believe You Can Catch Up

Mara was overwhelmed; she juggled school, work, and family commitments. At one point she asked, "When is our next exam?"

"Next Thursday."

"Oh no! I'm going to have to catch up with my reading this weekend. I haven't read anything since the last exam."

"That was four weeks ago!"

"I know, but I've been so busy."

I bet I can guess what happened that weekend: as she sat down to "catch up," Mara saw that she had 104 pages to read and then she freaked out. She was so jacked up with anxiety that she couldn't even concentrate on what she was reading. And the following Thursday, she tanked the exam.

I'm always surprised when students try to read more than one chapter in their textbook in a single weekend. Textbooks are boring. Often they downright suck. Which is why good students know to study a little at a time to make it manageable. If it was impossible to choke through a chapter a week ago, why does it seem likely that you'll be able to manage two this week?

39 Cheat

Donna and David sat together at the back of the classroom. Donna finished her exam a good fifteen minutes ahead of David and then sat her exam right side up on the edge of her desk and waited for David to finish. I wondered to myself, "Does she think I'm an idiot? That I just don't care? That I am too big of a wimp to do anything about their blatant cheating?" But for now, I don't say anything, I just watch in amazement.

It is now the next class meeting, and Donna and David sit together in my office.

"Do you know why I've asked you to see me?"

"No," says David

Donna shakes her head.

"You guys cheated on your exam."

"No we didn't," says David determined to carry his bluff all the way.

"I watched you cheat. You didn't even try to hide it. Donna set her exam out in plain sight and I watched you look at it and mark answers on your own exam."

"We didn't," from David again. Donna looks like she might puke.

"Yes, you did. If you admit to it we can talk about what is going to happen to you."

A long pause and then, "We are boyfriend and girlfriend. We work together." No remorse whatsoever.

"Later are you planning on sharing one transcript? One college degree?"

"You can't prove we cheated! It's your word against ours!" cries Donna.

"Not exactly, it's your word against statistics."

"What?"

"I ran a statistical analysis on your errors. The probability of your identical errors happening by chance is less than $1/1000^{th}$ of a percent. You have a greater chance of getting struck by lighting twice in the same spot. Would you like to walk with me to the dean's office, and you can argue your word against mine?"

"Now what are we supposed to do? We can't afford to get an F on our transcripts. We are going to drop the class."

"You won't be allowed to drop because I am turning in an incident report—you will receive a letter grade in the course. You can either work really hard on the next exam to get a better grade or leave and take an F."

Donna and David made some big mistakes, one right after the next:

1. They cheated.
2. They denied cheating.
3. They were angry at being caught and not at all remorseful.
4. They assumed beforehand they could talk their way out of it if they were caught.
5. They underestimated me (I am a trained anticheating professional).

Donna and David made a big mistake in assuming that if caught they'd just "deny, deny, deny." In any "student said/instructor said" situation, the instructor usually wins. If you want me to walk with you to the dean's office to give it a shot, though, I'm more than happy to go with you. If it was your first offense and you apologize profusely, I usually give you an F on the exam and allow you to continue in the course—you can still pass the class if you reform your ways. However, if you go to the dean with your denials, then I am forced to turn in an incident report.

Our college policy indicates that it is up to the instructor's discretion whether to turn in a cheater to the higher powers. And if I turn in an incident report, you can't drop the class. You get a big, fat F for your troubles and a big red cheater stamp in your permanent file.

STRATEGIES FOR SUCCESSFUL STUDENTS

- Read for comprehension
- Once you have a good grasp of the material you're ready to work on remembering it
  - ❑ Make concept maps
  - ❑ Build retrieval cues into the concept map
  - ❑ Seek out study resources to use as short cuts: supplements, online
- Study actively using retrieval practice
  - ❑ Relate the information to your own life
  - ❑ Distribute your studying
  - ❑ Use mnemonics
  - ❑ Overlearn the material
- Develop good test-taking practices
  - ❑ Work with a professional to reduce "real" test anxiety if needed
  - ❑ Read directions carefully
  - ❑ Do your own work
- Make use of study materials provided by the professor and/or textbook publisher

EXERCISE 3.1   *Exam Preparation Plan*

Choose one of your classes this semester and answer the following questions.

When is the next exam?

What chapters does it cover?

What format is the exam (e.g., multiple choice, essay)?

Which of the following supplemental resources are available to help you study?
- ☐ Workbook
- ☐ CD-ROM tutorials
- ☐ Instructor's study guide
- ☐ Companion website

How much time will be necessary to study for the exam?

How can you distribute your time over several weeks rather than cramming?

Which of the following campus resources may be necessary for you to do well on the exam?
☐ Psychological services to deal with motivational or anxiety issues
☐ Tutoring to help with mastery of course material
☐ Child care services to watch the rug rats so I can study
☐ Health center
☐ Computer center
☐ Library

What study techniques will you use?
☐ Mnemonics
☐ Flash cards
☐ Inspiration software
☐ Cheating (check this and you automatically fail!)

EXERCISE 3.2   Memory Tools

Point your Internet browser at www.mindtools.com and use the information in the memory portion of that website to answer the following questions.

Describe how you could use one technique for memorizing an ordered list of 10 items (e.g., the articles in the U.S. Bill of Rights, the cranial nerves etc. . .).

Describe how to use concept maps and draw a concept map for one of your current classes.

Identify and describe one additional technique that might be helpful to you in one of your current classes.

EXERCISE 3.3   Reflection

Please use the following space to reflect on what you've learned from this chapter, and how it can be applied to your life.

Basic Skills and Assignments

Ineptitude: if you can't learn to do something well, learn to enjoy doing it poorly.

—www.despair.com

One semester, my students were required to do a weekly assignment that consisted of watching a brief video clip and answering some simple questions about it. It was really an easy assignment. However, Roland complained to me, "Those videos are too difficult for foreign students to understand."

"What do you mean?"

"If you don't speak English then they don't make sense."

"Uh, probably not. You do need to be able to speak and comprehend English to succeed in this class, though."

"That isn't fair."

"How is that unfair? I took French for six years, yet I wouldn't go sit in a college class in Paris and complain because nothing made sense to me. I know my own limitations—I'd probably have to go to one of their elementary schools to have a fighting chance. We've got a great English as a Second Language (ESL) program; maybe you should take some of those classes and take this class when you've improved your language skills."

"It doesn't seem right. You shouldn't have to speak English to pass this class."

Roland must be out of his mind! The ability to comprehend the language in which instruction is delivered is just one of the basic competencies that you must have before attempting college courses. College professors expect you to be able to read, write, and think critically and analytically. The current chapter shows you that without a solid foundation in basic skills like reading, writing, and math you will flunk out of college for sure.

40 Cultivate Excuses

As far as excuses go, Lisa's is still my all-time favorite. A week before a major term paper was due she said, "I won't be able to finish my paper by the due date. Is it okay if I turn it in late?"

"As it says in the syllabus, you can turn it in one day late, but you only get half credit."

"I was sort of hoping I could turn the paper in *next semester*. Is there some way to get an incomplete because I'm getting married the day the paper is due?"

"You're getting *married* that day?" I ask, already thinking that if she knew she was going to be gone the day the paper was due, she should have planned to get the paper in early.

But she continued, "Actually, I'm not getting married on that day *this* year. I'm going to be getting married on that day *next* year."

"Huh? Now I'm totally confused."

"We want to celebrate that day as our prewedding anniversary. It's really important to us."

"That is one of the lamest excuses I have ever heard. Did you make that up?"

"No, I'm serious. I know it sounds crazy to anyone else, but our prewedding anniversary is special."

As a teacher, I've heard lots of excuses. Poor study habits and late assignments have been blamed on learning disabilities, difficult parents, kids, jobs, spouses, illness, poor English language skills and even the family dog. Just when I think that I've heard every possible excuse, a new one like Lisa's comes along.

While these personal issues do come up—I don't necessarily think that students are lying about them—*they are still just excuses*. Everyone has responsibilities outside of school, and everyone faces occasional surprises or emergencies. Still, part of success in college, as in life, means that you must learn to expect the unexpected to arise and develop study habits that include a sort of "insurance policy" against such eventualities.

What do I mean by insurance? *Effective time management*. For example, you should work on papers gradually over the course of the semester rather than begin them a day or two before they're due. And studying a week or two in advance of a test can work wonders to ameliorate last-minute crises.

If you wait until the last minute to complete an assignment and a crisis arises, then you have an important decision to make. You either

1. Stop and deal with the crisis, or
2. Ignore the crisis and study as planned.

If the crisis is something major—a death in the family, serious illness, or other emergency—then you need to stop and deal with it. However, you should realize that stopping to deal with the emergency may mean losing points on an assignment. Look at your professor's policy (as written in the syllabus). He or she may have a "no late homework policy," in which case by remaining in the class after the first class session (when the syllabus is distributed and explained), you must be prepared to live with the consequences of turning in a late paper. Likely this means getting a zero and lowering your grade in the course, or possibly dropping the course and retaking it at a better time in your life. Accept that you may not always have it both ways; that is, remaining in a class with a "no late homework" policy and then demanding a makeup assignment if you encounter an emergency.

If your professor has a strict policy about late assignments or missed exams, then any attempts from you to garner sympathy from her for a last-minute emergency will likely fall on deaf ears because she expected you to spend weeks preparing the assignment. It amazes me when a student says to me, "I meant to study for the exam, I swear, but the night before the exam I had to take my mom to the hospital." Whoa! Did you just admit you planned all along to wait until the day before the exam to begin studying?

Your professor is a person, too. He has dealt with household or family emergencies, deaths, sickness, you name it, and yet he still shows up for work and performs to the best of his abilities. For example, I remember the day in graduate school I was running experiments early in the morning; that afternoon I went to the dentist to have all my wisdom teeth pulled. As soon as I was out of the dentist's chair, I went right back to the lab to finish running my experiments. I didn't want to do it, but such experiments, once begun, must be run to their completion or abandoned, so I dealt with the hardships and got my job done. That is what competent professionals do.

41 Avoid Taking Math Until the Last Possible Semester

Ginny was a community college student who mentioned in passing that she hated math so much that she was going to postpone taking it for as long as possible. I knew she was making a mistake, so I asked her:

"What math course did you place in when you took the placement exam?"

"This is really embarrassing, but I placed in the basic arithmetic class."

"That's not unusual. Most students here need to take a refresher course or two before they are ready for college-level math."

"I told you I was bad at math."

"I'm only concerned because if you wait to take math, you won't be able to take enough math courses to meet the entry requirements for your transfer institution."

"No biggie, I'll just wait and take it there."

"It doesn't work that way. You need to complete those courses first or you won't get into the university."

"I'm sure it will work out."

"It will only 'work out' if you start taking math in the upcoming semester and keep taking it until you're ready to transfer."

If you hate math, it's easy to avoid. However, many top universities will not admit you or allow you to graduate without calculus. If you haven't mastered basic math, then you may be five or more classes away from completing this requirement. If you ignore it, you may finish all your other transferable courses yet be stuck at the community college for another *two years* just taking math courses!

So what should you do? Start taking a simple math class early and take math every semester while you're completing your general education. It never hurts and always makes you competitive when you apply to transfer institutions.

42 Say, "I'm Just Hoping to Pass My Current Math Class"

It was the week before final exams when I overheard two students talking.

"I'm just hoping to pass my math class. I don't want to have to take it again."

"I know, I had to take *Math 100* three times. I hated it!"

"Oh, I hope that doesn't happen to me. I just need to get an 85% on the final to pull off a C in the class."

"That isn't too bad."

"I hope not. I only need one more math class after this one and I want to get it over with."

If you struggle with math (and if you do, you're certainly not alone), it's tempting to rejoice when you finally pass a math class. The problem is, *each math course builds off the last one*. It makes little sense to move on to the next course until you have mastered the previous one. And when I say mastery, I really mean 90% or better proficiency. Yikes!

You ought to begin by taking refresher courses, enlist the aid of a good math tutor, and spend as many hours as is necessary to ace the course. If necessary, cut back on your total units that semester. If you do that for a semester or two, you'll likely discover that math gets easier with practice.

I have to confess that math has never been *my* strongest subject. My own struggles with the subject began in elementary school when, to my humiliation, I was the only student who had to leave the fifth grade class at math time to join the fourth graders! I struggled with math all the way through school until I got to college.

When I started college, I took a placement exam that placed me in intermediate algebra. However, I realized that to transfer to my preferred university, I was going to need to pass calculus. To get one step closer to the required calculus, many students would rush to take intermediate algebra; however, I actually enrolled in elementary algebra because I wanted to master the basics to avoid getting behind in intermediate algebra. Since I'd had elementary algebra in high school, I aced the college version (it was even—dare I say—a little *too easy*). But by taking the refresher course, I accomplished two things:

1. I felt triumphant at my success for the first time in a math class and
2. It made taking intermediate algebra a lot easier.

I aced intermediate algebra, then trigonometry, and then calculus. I got A's in them all! This was certainly not because I'm gifted at math, rather it's because I forced myself to master the basics before moving on. Had I gotten a C in intermediate algebra, I may have failed calculus.

I'm still not a math whiz, but I know I can take any course—graduate school involved a bunch of statistics courses—and survive. Trust me, if I can do it, anyone can!

43 Ignore Placement Exams

If you let your ego get in the way of your success, you may decide to enroll in a course that is more advanced than your recommended placement level. Denny made this mistake when transferring from one college to another. In high school, Denny had taken a beginning algebra class, with limited success. In college, Denny's test scores placed him in *Elementary Algebra*. However, he somehow convinced his professor that he had already successfully taken *Elementary Algebra* elsewhere and so was allowed to enroll in *Intermediate Algebra*.

Denny drowned in the intermediate course. He felt like a failure and ended up having to retake both *Elementary* and *Intermediate Algebra*. Not only did Denny waste the time he was trying to save by jumping ahead, he set himself up for failure and the associated feelings of incompetence that go with it.

44 Ignore Prerequisites

I teach an online version of *Introduction to Psychology;* it requires considerable computer literacy before registering for the course. On the first day of class, I discussed the computer requirement and asked if anyone was going to have a problem with it.

Dina said, "I might have a problem. The last time I used anything resembling a computer was twenty years ago and it was a typewriter."

"If that is the case, then I strongly recommend that you take the regular *Introduction to Psychology* course instead of the online version."

"I'd really like to try this class. I think I can do it. I'm a quick learner."

"Honestly, I don't think anyone, no matter how bright, can master the nuances of computing at the same time that he or she's trying to take an online class. You'd be better off taking the regular class with me in conjunction with an *Introduction to Computers* class."

"I'd still like to try this class."

So Dina tried—and she failed. Forget not being able to complete the assignments; by the middle of the semester, she had not even been able to get *into* the course Web site! By then, she had missed more than half of the homework and quizzes.

When a course has a prerequisite (a course you need to have completed prior to the current course), the teacher will assume that you have already gained a working knowledge of the material in that required course. If you try to skip these requirements, you will more than likely fail (and lose a semester's worth of work besides).

Never take a class in which you have a high probability of failure! It only creates disillusionment with college and learning in general. Instead, set yourself up for success by taking classes that are compatible with your current knowledge and skills.

45 Expect Graders to Be Mind Readers

Some students dislike writing so much that they finish writing a paper, pull it out of the printer, and turn it in immediately just so they don't ever have to look at it again. If you do this, you'll never know whether you said what you intended to say in the paper. For instance, consider the following journal entry by a student named Clyde:

> People have always been curious of how different mammals speak (communicate). The study of sounds within a dolphins cackles (screeching), has not been completely defined, but some of the sounds btw the pod as a whole has; when studying diff mammals of the sea, it has been defined to study the whole populace, to vary degrees of gestures, unspoken language, and the spoken language of the pod. Because as you watch their behavior, the spoken language of screeches, hums, and snorts, as all language is defined with attn to a single dolphin, whale, or primate to how they react, developed behavior, to corroborate what is being said.

Did this paragraph make any sense to you? I couldn't make heads or tails of it. Many students, like Clyde, make the mistake of assuming the teacher will understand what you were *trying* to say. However, when I read your paper, I have to look at what you *actually* said. It's the only objective piece of information that I have. I'm not a mind reader, so I won't make guesses about what you *meant* to say.

If he had written this entry a lot sooner, let a few days pass, and then went back to read what he had written, then Clyde might have seen that his entry makes little sense. At that point, he could have rewritten the paper to make it clearer. It's also clear that Clyde doesn't know how to use a spell-checker or other similar tools. These mistakes can be costly in terms of your overall grade.

46 Avoid Proofreading

If Clyde had been willing to do one additional step, he could have improved his paper even more—by letting someone else proofread his paper. He could have enlisted another student in the class, a friend, a sibling, or a writing center tutor to provide feedback on his paper *before* he turned it in. That way, someone else might identify problems that might result in a lower grade.

On the day that my *Research Methods* class had their second of four papers due, I surprised the class by saying, "We will spend this period reading each other's papers and using my grading checklist to edit them. You'll then have one additional day to rewrite and improve your papers." I did this for a reason. I wanted students to see firsthand the advantage of having someone else proofread for them.

The class let out a cry of joy.

"A second chance!" someone said.

"Dr. Cannon doesn't usually give second chances, so let's grade the *s*^ *@ out of these papers!" said another.

Afterward, everyone agreed that the activity was productive. Not only did students get their papers pre-graded, they learned by grading others' papers and seeing what their classmates did right or wrong.

Adam was a good writer who also turned out to be an especially talented editor. He ended up reading papers for not one but three of his peers that day, and pointed out bunches of costly errors in each of his peers' papers. He was thanked profusely. I was sure everyone would want Adam to do their pre-grading next time.

Just before the third paper was due, I told students that there wouldn't be a formal opportunity to pre-grade papers. If they felt the activity was beneficial—and they all said that it was—then they were encouraged to complete their papers a day or two early and trade with another student.

Not one person did it. The scores on the third paper were lower than the second paper and I poured red ink all over those papers. Wouldn't it be better to have someone else help you fix your paper before I got my hands on it?

47 Plagiarize

Kathy and Kyle did everything together. They took all the same classes, studied together, and worked on homework assignments together.

I was grading homework assignments and noticed that Kathy had a peculiar typing style. She would cApitalize the sEcond letter of many words. She thought it was "cute." I thought it was annoyingly difficult to read.

When I got to Kyle's homework and saw that he had cApitalized the sEcond letter of the same words as Kathy, I *knew*—one of them did the homework and the other just printed out a second copy of it. Can you wave the proverbial red "cheater" flag any more obviously than this? Some students must think my mom dropped me on my head when I was a baby.

What Kathy and Kyle did was a form of plagiarism (using another person's words or ideas without giving them credit). If you want to get labeled with the "P" word, do one of the following:

- Copy someone's words verbatim and forget to put quotes around it
- Fail to cite the sources of ideas
- Copy a chart, graph, or illustration without citing the source
- Paraphrase by just rearranging or changing a few words while keeping the main idea
- Combine your own words with passages cut and pasted from various Web sites
- Have someone else write your paper or complete your assignment

By definition, it doesn't matter if plagiarism is intentional or accidental. If you plan to plagiarize and then say, "It was an accident," this won't be enough to save you. Plagiarism is plagiarism. You'll likely still fail the assignment, and you will deserve what you get.

The Internet makes stealing a paper easier than ever—you can go online and purchase a term paper for about $4.95 a page. If you're thinking that this is a great resource for students, consider this: *resources for teachers are even better.* There are software robots that endlessly crawl the Internet twenty-four hours a day, compiling information that teachers can use to identify stolen papers. It will be less effort (and less expensive) for your teacher to catch you cheating than for you to cheat.

Furthermore, if a student writes a brilliant (and therefore suspicious) paper, then he or she may be asked to write on demand to prove that it's his or her writing. If you're suddenly at a loss for intelligent prose, then you're toast.

Once you get caught, you have destroyed your entire academic career and flunked out of college using just *one* of my tips. Congratulations!

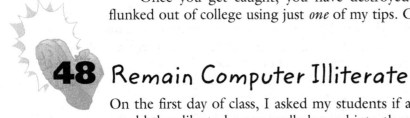

48 Remain Computer Illiterate

On the first day of class, I asked my students if anyone was a computer novice and would they like to be personally logged into the course Web site and shown how to access the documents. The rest of the class would be able to view the login process, but that person would learn firsthand.

Judy said she was willing to be a guinea pig because she had no idea how to use a computer. Everyone else indicated they had at least a passing familiarity with computers, so Judy was up.

After the demonstration, I told Judy to feel free to stop by my office a few times if she had any questions or needed help accessing the Web site but Judy went and dropped the class that same day.

The next semester, Judy was back on the first day of class. I was surprised, and delighted that she was willing to give the class another go. But, she wasn't there to try it again. Instead, she said, "Does anyone want to buy the textbook for this class? I bought the book for it and won't be taking it because I don't want to use a computer."

The class looked at her like she was from Mars. No one bought the book from her. So she left.

"What was her problem?" Christy asked.

"I just think she isn't familiar with computers and I don't think she wants to learn to use one."

"What if she needs to use one in a job one day?" Mike asked.

Thanks, Mike. My point exactly.

I don't suggest, I *demand* that students use a computer. Why? It's important for students to have what educators like to call *information competency.* This is the ability to use the Internet as a research tool, to do simple searches and to retrieve documents. Computers aren't going away, so get comfortable with them! Basic computing abilities are indispensable in today's job market. Without them, you will be at a huge disadvantage.

49 Don't Be a Reader

Many students are unprepared for the heavy reading load that is required in college. Recently, I was in our college bookstore and overheard a student say, "I am only taking four classes. Why do I have to buy ten books? I'm never going to be able to read any of this stuff."

"Yeah, I don't even know why I am buying these books," said another student, "I never even cracked one of my books last semester. It's such a waste."

In class, that same day, one of my own students asked, "Do I really need to read the book?"

"No. The assigned textbook is only for those students who want to pass my class."

There are always a handful of students for whom the textbook is nothing more than an overpriced paperweight. Most students merely skim the book while a relative few engage in active reading strategies. Take Jennifer, for example:

"I read the chapter but when I was finished I didn't remember anything from it."

"What did you do to try and remember what you read?"

"What do you mean?"

"As you were reading, what strategies did you use to help ensure you'd remember the material?"

"I don't know. I guess none. I'm just not a reader."

"You should drop out then."

"You think I should drop your class?"

"No, I think you should drop all your classes. Quit college and do something else."

"No way, I want to get a good job some day."

"Then you need to become a reader."

I can't think of a single job where reading isn't important. You need to read to be an informed citizen, to keep up with advances in your field, and to succeed in your career. Before you ever land that great job though, you'll need to read a great deal of information to survive your college experience.

Those students who do read effectively and survive have books that look like disaster survivors. The spines are bent from heavy use, there are markings and drawing on the pages, key words are highlighted, and questions are written in the margins. As good readers, they actively search for potential exam questions as they read.

STRATEGIES FOR SUCCESSFUL STUDENTS

- Get immediate help for math anxiety
- Master the basics before moving forward
- Take a study skills course
- Practice, practice, practice basic skills like writing and math
- Write papers, edit, rewrite, proofread, and then rewrite them
- Improve your computer literacy
- Develop your reading skills

Name: _____   **Date:** _____

EXERCISE 4.1   Requirements for Graduation

For this exercise you will need to choose a college major. If you already know what you want to major in, choose that major. Otherwise, choose a subject that is interesting enough to you to complete this assignment.

What is your major? _____
In order to obtain a degree in this major, what courses must you complete?

What are the prerequisites for the above courses?

Go to two Web sites for two potential transfer or graduate institutions and identify the graduation requirements for an additional degree in your major.

Institution name

University One	University Two

What is the minimum level of math needed for graduation?

University One	University Two

What are the minimum English course requirements needed for graduation?

University One	University Two

What additional courses are required for your major?

University One	University Two

What prerequisites are required for entrance into the above courses?

Univerity One	University Two

EXERCISE 4.2   Basic Skills Self-Analysis

The three California public higher education institutions worked together and came up with a list of basic skills that are expected from college freshman. Point your internet browser to *http://www.getreallearning.com/Academic_Literacy__A_Statement_of_Competencies_Expected_of_ Students_Entering.pdf* for a paper describing the skills they've identified as necessary for college success.

For each of the 6 skills below, describe the steps you could take to improve in that area. Be specific!

1. Habits of Mind

2. Understanding the connection between reading and writing

3. Reading

4. Writing

5. Listening and Speaking

6. Technology

EXERCISE 4.3 Reflection

Please use the following space to reflect on what you've learned from this chapter, and how it can be applied to your life.

CHAPTER 5

Time Management

It's ironic that every year new time saving gadgets are invented, yet increasingly people in many contexts seem to say, "I don't have enough time." Do you exercise regularly? "Not enough time." Do you keep your room, apartment, or house clean? "No time." Did you study for your midterm? "Too busy." But is it really a lack of time that plagues us, or are our priorities skewed? If I said, "If you exercise three times this week for at least a half hour at a time, I'll give you $10,000," then you'd make the time. If your roommate paid you $500 each week that your clothes were kept off the floor, you'd do it. If I gave all students who got an A in my course a million bucks, I'd suddenly get a bunch of people who "found" more time to study.

Our perception of time is relative. In college I worked as a research assistant for a graduate student: I photocopied articles for her, organized her files, and so on. We each benefited: I learned a few things about conducting research and she got cheap labor. After doing this for a semester, I felt I'd learned about all I could from the assignment and told my boss that I didn't have enough free time to continue as her research assistant the following semester. She nearly fell out of her chair laughing, "You don't have time? Wait until *you* go to graduate school!"

I was perplexed until I started graduate school myself, whereupon I found I was now expected to do everything I did as a college student while at the same time running laboratory experiments, serving as a teaching assistant, and writing up my research reports for publication. As a college student, I probably worked thirty hours a week; I now worked as many as eighty hours per week. In retrospect, I realize that my workload increased every year from my freshman year through the culmination of my doctorate. By the time I was in my last year in the doctoral program, I too laughed at college students who had "too little time."

The current chapter describes strategies that you can use to waste the one non-replenishing resource that you have: Time. When it's gone, it's gone forever.

50 Don't Take Study Breaks

I had a college roommate named Angela who studied constantly. Day or night, if she wasn't sleeping, showering, or eating, she was studying. I'd study for an hour or two and then take a break, but Angela was still going strong.

One day I had been studying for a killer *Psycholinguistics* midterm and decided to take a break from my studies and go to the mall. I asked Angela, "Do you want to go shopping?"

"No, I'm studying."

"I know, but don't you want to take a break for a while?"

"No, thanks. Shouldn't *you* be studying, too?"

"I studied for two hours already, and I'll get back to it later but I just need a break to clear my head."

"I don't know about you, but I plan on doing well on my midterms," she said condescendingly.

"So do I. That's why I need to get away for a few hours."

A few days later, I'd ask, "Hey, want to go to the movies?"

"Sorry, I have too much studying to do. Why aren't you studying?"

"I was, I just needed an escape for a couple hours."

As midterms rolled around she got Cs and I got As. Does this seem strange? Why did I get better grades than Angela? It's simple—I was a better and more efficient student. She waited until a week or two before exams and then studied around the clock. I spread out my studying over the course of the term and I never spent more than a couple of hours studying without taking a break to do something fun. I'd study math, then read a magazine. I'd hit the books and review for philosophy class and then grab a bite to eat. After practicing French, I'd spend time with friends.

By distributing my effort I never felt too burdened by my studies—because a little studying was always rewarded with something fun. And because I had already studied, the fun was guilt-free! I was willing to make sacrifices for good grades, but I recognized the need to reward my efforts as well. And besides, as a psych major I knew any behavior that is followed by a reward is likely to increase.

There is a common misconception that straight A students aren't having fun or partying as much as C students are. I'll let you in on a secret: most straight A students are having just as much fun as you, they just arrange their schedule so their fun always follows a bit of hard work. Like you, they know that life is too short not to have a little fun. But perhaps unlike you, they know that if they finished college, then they'd have a higher paying job and ultimately more freedom to do the activities they love.

51 *Act Like a Pigeon*

Consider the following questions:

- Do you arrange your school schedule around your social life?
- Do you plan vacations or activities that conflict with your studies?
- At the end of the day do you find yourself saying, "Darn, I didn't get anything productive done today!"

If you answered, "yes" to one or more of the above questions, then you're behaving more like a pigeon than an intelligent human being.

Let me explain. I spent years studying pigeons, who pressed keys (with their beaks) for food rewards, and those birds behave exactly the same way. Okay, so pigeons aren't exactly hanging out with friends or doing the same things you do, but what they are doing is choosing an activity that leads to a small immediate reward (e.g., pecking a key that leads to an immediate but small piece of food) over an activity that leads to a larger but delayed reward (e.g., pecking a key a little longer for a large amount of food).

At first glance, the pigeon's behavior seems rational: if he pecks the small-reward key he gets the payoff *now* whereas the future is sometimes uncertain (at least from the bird's point of view). However, if you look at the long-term consequences it doesn't seem so rational; over the long run, the pigeon typically wastes considerable energy for less food overall. Pigeons presumably can't exercise self-control (and wait for a larger portion of food) because they can't relate their current behavior to the future.

However humans (even the dumbest ones) have a greater mental capacity than pigeons: they can use their knowledge and reasoning skills to exercise self-control. For instance, I was about to order dessert at a fancy restaurant when the waiter suggested a chocolate soufflé that takes about a half-hour to make. If I ordered one of the other desserts, I could have it immediately, but none of the other desserts were chocolate. Can I wait a little longer for chocolate? You bet I can! We're talking CHOCOLATE!

The reason most of you went to college in the first place was to get a higher-paying job some day. To get the job, you need the degree, and to get the degree you need the grades. In college, grades are sometimes not delivered until weeks or months after an exam or assignment has been turned in, and the degree itself can take four to six years to complete. And it could be a decade before any real money comes rolling in.

Like the pigeon, your rewards for going to college are delayed and you may have trouble connecting those future rewards (higher paying job ten years from now) to your current behavior (studying). Therefore, it isn't surprising if you engage in activities like watching TV, shopping, or playing sports to the detriment of your studies. These activities are rewarding *right now.*

However, playing when you should be studying comes with costs. The long-term costs are obvious: bad grades, failure, and lower wages. These costs are easy to discount because they won't become apparent until the future. However, there are some current costs as well. If you're out enjoying a concert, shopping, or watching a movie, your enjoyment of the activity is sometimes interrupted by a little voice that whispers relentlessly: *"You should be studying right now!"* Somehow the little voice always manages to diminish your fun with a bad case of anxiety and guilt.

 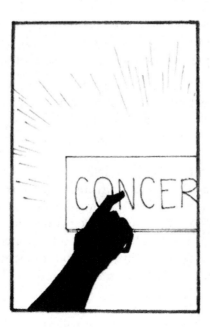 

ryanwinn.com

One of the best ways to prevent unnecessary stress is through better time management. Imagine going out with your tasks out of the way. Wouldn't your fun, be, well, more fun? If you did a little homework and then went out, it would be. Once I discovered that studying alleviated most of the anxiety associated with not studying, I became hooked on studying. If I wanted to go out and have fun? I knew that if I studied a little and then went out, I could tell the little voice to be quiet because I had already studied. Eventually I worked out a deal with the little voice—I'll study a little now, then go out, then study a little more. It stopped nagging me after that.

So if you want to act like a human and not a "rat with wings," use a little self-control when you make current decisions that affect your future.

52 Procrastinate

I received a funny email from Derek:

"I'm sorry I'm sending this so late, but here is my self-modification project proposal entitled 'Putting An End To Procrastination.'"

That's hilarious! Doesn't he see the irony?

Procrastination (putting off for tomorrow what you should be doing today) is a common problem among students. Do you wait till the night before a test to begin studying? Do you stay up all night writing papers the day before they are due? If so, then you're a procrastinator.

Procrastination is a great way to fail in college, because it helps you to maximize the impact of deaths, illness, and emergencies that inevitably arrive the day before a big assignment is due. It's as if the world knows you're unprepared. A paper is due tomorrow? Your printer craps out. You planned to spend the entire night studying for tomorrow's test? Your little brother needs a ride to the emergency hospital. Your professors know these crises arise, but they expect you to plan for potential emergencies and budget extra time into your study plan. *Your* emergency is not *their* emergency.

I suspect that one of the biggest reasons students procrastinate is they mistakenly believe that they need to be "in the mood" to do their homework or study for exams. These students put comfort first. They make self-statements such as:

- I don't feel like doing my paper now, I'll do it tomorrow
- I'm not in the mood to study, I'll study later
- This chapter is too long, I'll read it another day when I have more energy

The erroneous assumption behind these statements is that tomorrow, later, or another day, you will feel like doing the work. But face it: have you ever woken up with a burning urge to study and forego everything you'd planned for that day? You assume that tomorrow you might be in a mood to study, when in reality the mood may never strike.

So if you don't feel like studying, what should you do? Study anyway! That's right, *even if you don't feel like studying, do it anyway!*

Okay, you see the problem, now how do you overcome it? Easy—start by taking baby steps. For instance, tell yourself you'll allow yourself to spend the rest of the day doing whatever you feel like after you have spent a half-hour to one-hour studying. Do this every day, increasing the amount of study time by ten minutes a day until you can handle an hour or two at a time, and you'll be ahead at test time.

53 Be Disorganized

Matt walked in just as I was passing out exams and giving last-minute instructions. He looked around the room, looked at me, and seemed, well, befuddled. Slowly, however, his confusion was replaced by panic: "Oh, *no*! There is an exam today? Why didn't anyone tell me?"

Nothing is more painful than seeing an unprepared student enter the class, look around the room and suddenly realize that there is an exam. Typically, said student arrives late, has no pencil and no *Scantron* form and must scramble around campus to purchase these necessities. Now he or she is not only unprepared but also wracked with anxiety as he settles in to take the exam.

How could this happen? Typically a disorganized student like Matt:

- Has lost important handouts
- Doesn't know the important dates
- Doesn't realize that it's *his* responsibility to keep track of important dates
- Expects verbal reminders from the professor

It's *your* job to keep track of handouts and be aware of important dates. College professors don't always give out verbal reminders in class. They believe they are teaching responsible adults.

Careless and disorganized students are likely to be plagued with problems throughout their professional lives. They "grow up" to become dentists who lose important client records (and consequently clients) or lawyers who are late to trial and receive sanctions from judges. Any high-paying, high-status job will require organization on your part, so you'd best acquire that skill now.

Students who immediately transfer important dates (i.e., exams, papers due) to their day planners and file their important handouts (i.e., syllabus, course calendar) in a three-ring binder just do better than students who are careless managers of this information.

54 Assume Waking Up Is Optional

On Monday, Brad apologized for missing last Wednesday's class.

"I just couldn't wake up," he admitted.

"Really? I had trouble waking on Wednesday myself. I did manage to make it to class on time, though."

Brad laughed and said, "Well, *duh,* you have to come to class because you're the teacher."

"I'm not sure I understand. Why do you have any less responsibility to show up than I do?"

"The teacher has to be here," says Brad, "but the students don't have to come."

"Where is that written?"

"I don't know if it's written anywhere, that's just how it is."

I agree with Brad that it's my job, as a teacher, to show up for my classes. However, I also believe that it's Brad's job, as a student, to show up for his classes. We each have a job to do. Contrary to Brad's belief, nothing bad will happen to me if I miss an occasional class (assuming I call in sick ahead of time). I will still get my usual salary, the president of the college will still say "hi" to me in the hallway, I will still keep my office, and my role as department chair is secure. However, if Brad misses class, then he will never be able to make up the missed material.

While I do sympathize with the need for adequate sleep, and I realize that some students are taking classes while also working and managing families, they still need to come to class. In fact, the reason that I was sleepy on that same Wednesday morning was because I taught a night class on Tuesday until 10:05 p.m. However, since I arranged my schedule this way, I accepted the responsibility for showing up at my arranged times. After going through a semester or two like this, I admitted that this schedule was difficult and arranged to begin my Wednesday mornings no earlier than 11:00 a.m. The moral of the story is, you need to understand your own body and arrange your schedule accordingly.

Sleep researchers distinguish between "morning larks" and "night owls." Morning larks wake up early in the morning, ready to start the day—they may even be a tad too cheerful for the rest of us. Night owls are most active in the evening hours. They go to bed late, and if possible sleep into the afternoon. Most young adults are night owls. If you're a night owl, then take night classes. If you have to take morning classes, go to sleep earlier.

55 Practice Perfectionism

Vincent had a solid 89% average after the first three out of four exams. When I received his class drop slip in the mail I was concerned that something had happened, so I gave him a call.

"Hi Vincent, I noticed that you dropped my class, and was just calling to make sure you were all right."

"Hey, thanks for calling. I appreciate your concern. I did drop your class but nothing is wrong. Honestly, I just didn't want to get a B in it."

Stunned, I asked, "You dropped the class because you were getting a B?"

"Yeah, I want to go to law school so I need to get all As."

"Hmm. I see you've done all your homework, and you had nearly perfect attendance so you'd have received an A when all the points were added in together—especially if you did well on the last exam."

"Yeah, I just didn't want to chance it."

So how many of you reading this would like to punch Vincent? Unbelievable isn't it?

I've been on several college and graduate admissions committees and I know for a fact that a "W" is perceived as worse than a B. Many schools will convert the "W" to an F anyway and then recalculate your GPA. Just because your current school has a so-called "forgiveness policy" that allows you to ignore a few bad marks if you retake the class and get a better grade, this doesn't guarantee that other schools will treat those earlier grades the same way. Those marks usually stay on your transcript with a special notation saying they weren't included in the calculation of your GPA, but a simple calculator will fix that.

I believe it's a good idea to set high standards for yourself. However, if the standards are set so high (e.g., "I must receive all As") that you're sure to fail, then it's a mistake. I have since had at least a handful of students who dropped one of my courses because they were getting a B.

56 Get So Involved in Extracurricular Activities That You Fail Your Classes

Michael was in student government. He worked tirelessly on a campaign to raise money for the college, spoke with passion in front of influential members of the community, and received awards for his service.

When Michael received a prestigious award at graduation, a colleague turned to me and said, "Hey, he failed my literature class twice!"

"Really?" He'd failed two of my psychology classes that semester, too.

It's a great idea to get involved in on campus activities, be it club membership, athletics, the debate team, or student government (in fact, when students are highly involved in their schools they are more likely to persist in completing a degree). However, if you choose to participate in extracurricular activities, you need to keep track of your priorities: attending class is more important than selling baked goods in the quad for the chess club.

It's tempting to get overly involved in low-priority activities (e.g., club activities) because they are usually fun, whereas high-priority activities (e.g., studying for an exam) are associated with anxiety. You have likely learned to do low-priority activities to escape from the anxiety associated with doing high-priority activities. Once you recognize this bad habit, it becomes possible to deal with it. If you're using extracurricular activities as a way to avoid your less exciting schoolwork, then maybe a visit to the campus psychologist will help you learn better strategies for managing your anxiety.

57 Take More Units Than You Can Handle

We've all experienced the stress of biting off more than we could chew. If you have work or family commitments, then you've definitely experienced the associated stress of balancing these commitments with attending college. But if you consistently fall behind in your studies despite good time management, then you're doing too much.

When I began taking community college courses, I started out taking twelve units and increased my load by three units each semester until I could comfortably handle eighteen units. The semester that I transferred to a university, I assumed the work would be harder so I scaled back to twelve units, then increased from there until I could handle at least fifteen units.

If you're working full-time then you can probably only successfully handle three to six units a semester. If you work part-time you may want to take the smallest number of full-time units that is possible.

If you're in over your head, you have to ask yourself: "If I dropped one class that I'm bombing, will I be able to make higher grades in my other courses?" If the answer is yes, then drop one class, learn from your miscalculation, and plan your next semester more carefully.

58 Allow Inertia and Apathy to Dominate Your Life

Bill was trying to decide on a topic for his self-management project but he was at a loss. He asked me for some suggestions.

"Do you smoke?"

"Yes."

"A lot of students who have been thinking about quitting, use that as their project."

"Nah, I like smoking too much."

"Do you procrastinate with your schoolwork?"

"Yeah, but it doesn't bother me."

"Don't your grades suffer?"

"Yeah, but I don't really care what grades I get. I've never been really motivated."

"Would you like to get better grades, or maybe work on your motivation level?"

"No, I really don't care."

"How about exercising more or eating better? Is that something you feel you should work on?"

"Probably, because I'm fat and never exercise, but it doesn't bother me."

"Why are you even in this class? Or in school for that matter?"

"I don't know. It's just something to do for now. Except for your class, school kinda sucks."

Do you think school sucks? Think it's boring? Not worth your time? Maybe you naïvely think that if you just sit there for four years and do some minimum amount of work, you'll finally get out with a degree and be "free." Free to do what, I'm not sure. Free from ever having to read a book or write a report? Free from giving oral presentations? Free to get paid for sitting around, whining and doing nothing?

I've got news for you. If you hate reading, writing reports, or presenting in front of a group, then you should consider leaving college to do something you truly love. Because if you finish college, the best, highest paying jobs are going to demand that you continually read, write, and give presentations. That's right! You'll need to keep doing the same stuff in your career that you can't get motivated to do right now.

So what exactly are you doing in college? If you're like most students, you wanted a better job. We live in an information age where the best jobs employ people as knowledge workers. To stay ahead, you'll need to constantly learn new information and communicate your ideas to others. In addition, jobs increasingly disappear or become obsolete, so chances are whatever you do, you'll need to return to school again and again throughout your work life.

In a so-called "real job" you will often need to read or write when you aren't in the mood. Imagine, for example, that you're a lawyer planning to spend three months preparing for a trial, when suddenly the judge moves up the trial date to two weeks from now. You may be tired, angry, and under pressure, but you still need to perform to survive.

Some students assume school sucks for everyone. They see their classes as a sort of nightmare that they hope to somehow live through. As I write this, I'm teaching a summer class where a good number of students said they are in summer school to get out of school as soon as possible. What do they think is going to happen when they graduate? Maybe they expect to be handed a diploma and a million dollar reward. Don't they understand that life will only become more demanding?

Next time you're in class feeling sorry for yourself, look at the woman a few seats over from you. She loves learning and sees school as a series of challenges instead of obstacles. In the classes she doesn't love, she approaches the course the way she would a bitter pill; she plugs her nose and takes it anyway. She is going to win the scholarships, internships, and awards that you, with your attitude, are not.

59 Let Stress Get Out of Control

Lydia said, "Dr. Cannon, I'm glad I caught you. Remember last semester when we talked about stress management?"

"Yes."

"What were those techniques you told us about?"

"I mentioned a variety of techniques targeting physical, emotional, and cognitive aspects of stress—which techniques are you talking about?"

"Any of them—I'm really stressed out this semester and I need to do something, anything."

Lydia did look tired and edgy, for good reason. She was taking several difficult classes, working a full-time job where she was miserable, and had recently broken up with her boyfriend. She wasn't eating well or getting enough sleep. To make matters worse, Lydia was feeling out of control and uncertain about the future. I wished I could think of something to say that would magically alleviate some of her stress, but I couldn't.

Unfortunately, stress management techniques are not a band-aid that you slap on only when a crisis hits—they are a *way of life*. That is, in order for stress management techniques to be available and effective during times of stress, you need to begin developing them far in advance; that way, you'll be already be proficient at them when major stress appears.

What are some of the techniques? They fall into three main categories:

1. Managing your *body's reaction* to stress (e.g., eating healthy, getting enough sleep, exercising).
2. Changing how you *think* about stressful situations (e.g., letting go of perfectionism or other unhealthy mindsets).
3. Managing your *emotional reaction* to stressful situations (e.g., handling anger and frustration appropriately).

There are many ways to learn stress management techniques—by taking a *Stress Management* class, reading books, or from personal consultations with a psychologist. If you don't want to flunk out of college, start learning some techniques today.

STRATEGIES FOR SUCCESSFUL STUDENTS

- Identify your time wasters and make a plan to deal with them
- Set study goals and measurable objectives
  - ❏ Make semester, weekly, and daily to-do lists
  - ❏ Prioritize your to-do list and complete high priority items first
  - ❏ Break down large tasks into smaller, more manageable ones
  - ❏ Distribute your studying over time
  - ❏ Take study breaks
  - ❏ Develop and practice stress-management techniques

EXERCISE 5.1   Time Management

Develop a schedule for the semester that will allow you to complete your school, work, and other obligations successfully.

Hour	Monday	Tuesday	Wednesday	Thursday	Friday	Saturday	Sunday
7:00							
8:00							
9:00							
10:00							
11:00							
12:00							
1:00							
2:00							

Hour	Monday	Tuesday	Wednesday	Thursday	Friday	Saturday	Sunday
3:00							
4:00							
5:00							
6:00							
7:00							
8:00							
9:00							
10:00							
11:00							
12:00							

Name: _____   Date: _____

EXERCISE 5.2 *Semester Calendar*

Use the following calendars to plan out your semester. Include important dates such as exams and assignment due dates.

Month_____

Sun	Mon	Tue	Wed	Thu	Fri	Sat

Month_____

Sun	Mon	Tue	Wed	Thu	Fri	Sat

Month_____

Sun	Mon	Tue	Wed	Thu	Fri	Sat

Month_____

Sun	Mon	Tue	Wed	Thu	Fri	Sat

EXERCISE 5.3 Time Wasters

Identify the activities that interfere with your schoolwork, the number of hours spent doing these activities, and a brief plan for dealing with these distractions.

	Which activities interfere?	How many hours are spent doing these activities?	How can you deal with these activities in a way that allows you to succeed in school?
Social activities (e.g., friends and family)			
Personal hobbies (e.g., surfing the Internet, watching television, shopping)			

	Which activities interfere?	How many hours are spent doing these activities?	How can you deal with these activities in a way that allows you to succeed in school?
Personal necessities (e.g., sleeping, exercising, eating, running errands)			
Other obligations (e.g., work, commuting, clubs)			

EXERCISE 5.4 Reflection

Please use the following space to reflect on what you've learned from this chapter, and how it can be applied to your life.

Grades

> **Whining: if you expect to score points by whining, join a European soccer team.**
>
> —*www.despair.com*

Good or bad, your final transcript tells a story. Future universities, employers, or scholarship committees will read your story and form opinions of you based on your permanent record. They will make decisions about you as well: whether or not to admit you, hire you, or give you free money. What story will your transcript tell at the end of your college experience? Here are three examples:

- Nicole's story is a common one. She started off a bit shaky: many withdraws, several Fs, and a few passing grades. Her transcripts were nothing to brag about. Over her first three years in college, as she matured and discovered her interests, her grades gradually improved; she ended with a respectable 3.2 GPA. What story does Nicole's transcript tell? Ask anyone who has sat on a college or graduate admissions committee, and he or she will tell you this pattern is quite typical.
- Vincent's is a sad tale; he started out with high hopes for himself, his early grades were lousy, and after losing his confidence, he dropped out, never to be seen again. Likely, he will never show his transcripts to anyone. Unfortunately, this includes high-paying employers.
- Robin started out strong and ended strong, graduating with a 4.0 GPA and a shot at becoming the valedictorian of her graduating class. She was one of fewer than 10 (out of roughly 7,000) students who qualified at our college to be given the title "First In Her Class."

When all is said and done, those marks printed on your transcripts are permanent. This chapter will tell you how to earn grades so lousy you might even get a big "L" for "loser" stamped on the top of your permanent record.

60 Depend on Your Professor to Calculate Your Grades

Jack asked, "Dr. Cannon, can you tell me what my grade is in this class so far?"

"The scores are all posted on the course Web site."

"I know, but I'm not sure what my score means."

"Divide your score by the total and multiply by 100."

Blank stare. How can Jack not know how to compute a simple average?

It's your *professor's* responsibility to promptly return your individual scores to you and to give you the grading scale that he or she will use, but it's *your* responsibility to keep track of your scores and to know what they mean. If this means visiting the math tutors to help you compute your grades or your GPA, then do it.

For instance, I use a standard scale where 90% is an A, 80% is a B, 70% is a C, and so forth. Jack received an 86, 73, 90, and 84. He needs to add up those four scores and divide by the total number of points. In his case, Jack adds his scores together to get 333, then divides 333 by 400 and gets an average of 83%.

Jack's next question is, "What do I need to get on the final exam to get an A in the class?" To figure this out, he needs to subtract his total score from the score necessary to obtain the lowest possible A to find out how many points he'd need. This is 90% of 500 (the new total with the final exam) or 450. If you subtract 333 from 450 this equals 117%. Unfortunately, in Jack's case this is impossible. He cannot get a 117% on an exam. At this point in the semester, Jack can earn no higher than a B.

Before he asks, let's help Jack compute his GPA at semester's end. To do it, we need to be able to set up a table like the one below. Jack took 5 classes and earned an A or B in all of them. He needs to multiply the units for each class by the grade earned in that class (for example he got an A in Fitness 101 and it was worth 1 unit) using A = 4, B = 3, C = 2, and D =1 (sorry, an F is worthless)[1].

Class	Units	Grade	Grade Points
Fitness 101	1.00	A	4.00
English 100	3.00	B	9.00
Philosophy 110	3.00	B	9.00
Psychology 200	3.00	A	12.00
Math 100	4.00	B	12.00
TOTAL	14.00		46.00

Jack can now figure his GPA by dividing the *Total Grade Points* by the *Total Units.* In this case, Jack's GPA is 46.00/14.00 or 3.29.

61 Forget the Learning and Focus Only on the Grade

Morgan was a student with a very high GPA, yet she whined, "Some of the questions that were on the study guide were not on the exam! I wasted my time studying for those."

"You didn't 'waste your time' because *any* of the material on the study guides might have ended up on the exam."

---

1. Refer to your college catalog in case your institution uses a different point system (for example, some use A = 4.00, A– = 3.7, and so on).

"You shouldn't put stuff on the study guide that won't be on the test. It isn't fair to the students."

"That's ridiculous, Morgan. You're supposed to learn all the material that I cover. I only test you on about 5% of the material because statistics tells me that with a decent sample size, if you know 80% of the material on the exam, then you probably know 80% of the material we covered."

"I still think you're not being kind to your students."

In my mind I started thinking ahead to the next semester, when Morgan was transferring to a state university. I couldn't wait until she saw how easy she had it here in comparison. I wanted to tell her, "You know, next semester you'll have to study *everything* because you won't even get a study guide," but I kept quiet.

And then the following semester it happened! I got an email from Morgan saying, "The classes are impossible at the university. The professor's don't even tell you what is going to be on the exam."

Ha!

Some students are focused only on what will be on the exam and have no interest in learning. If this describes you, try to keep this a secret from your professors, who hope you have a passion for knowledge and learning for its own sake. Therefore, you should try to avoid asking any of the following questions:

- "Is this going to be on the test?"
- "Do I have to do this?"
- "Is this going to be graded?"
- "Can I get points for doing this?"

62 Try Coasting

I'll admit to it. In high school, I'd screw around all semester, kick in a bit of effort on the last exam, and pull off a passing grade. I passed doing this, and likely you did too, because your high school teachers were afraid—they were pressured by students, parents, administrators, and the community to pass students or chance looking like the school was doing a lousy job.

Guess what? As a college professor, I have NO FEAR! If I teach a class with fifty students and all fifty students get less than 50% of the total points, then everyone gets an F. Of course, I don't *want* that to happen and it never *has* happened (though one semester it came close) but that is beside the point. If I followed my syllabus, and had clear and explicit expectations, then I will apologize to no one for failing the entire class. So go ahead, try me.

On the first day of class last semester, I asked everyone to guess what the distribution of grades was on the first exam in the same class the previous semester. A few college-savvy students guessed that there was a bell-shaped curve; but they were wrong! Of the thirty-nine students who ultimately completed the class these were their scores on Exam 1:

- 0%   As
- 10%   Bs
- 13%   Cs
- 21%   Ds
- 56%   F's

I mentioned this in the current class because I was trying to help my new students avoid making one key mistake: assuming that without studying you may just get lucky and pass the first test.

My theory was that students try to take their first exam without studying for it, in the naïve attempt to get a good grade with no effort. I mean, if you could pass the class by doing nothing, why waste effort? When that fails, you kick in some minimum amount of effort in an attempt to bring up your earlier grade. The problem is, this strategy rarely works! The final grade distribution for the above students at the end of the term came in at:

- 3%   As
- 23% Bs
- 28% Cs
- 28% Ds
- 18% Fs

These numbers are a bit deceptive because most of the students who received Fs on the first exam dropped the course. In reality, the overall performance of the course improved only slightly. As you can see, the majority of students got a C or worse.

Maybe it's time you realize that if you try coasting early in the semester you will likely fail. However, imagine you're like Russell (he was the one and only person who got an A in the above course). He received a high B on Exam 1, and by the time he was going into the final exam he had a 96% average. He only needed a 66% on the final to maintain his A in the course. If anyone could have coasted at the end of the semester, it was Russell; he could have taken a break and studied a little less for the final to focus more on his other classes. What did he get on his final? A 94%! Way to go Russell!

63 Be a Grade Grubber

I've just shown you how students who blow off studying for an entire semester, only to kick in a bit of effort at the end, mostly fail. Yet incredibly, some of these students believe they should get the grade they *wanted* rather than the grade they *deserved*. They naively believe that in lieu of actually earning the grade they wanted, they can try to scrape together missing points and if that doesn't work, beg:

- "Is there anything I can do to improve my grade?"
- "I think I deserve more points on this assignment."
- "I don't think this score is fair. I believe this paper is worth more points."
- "Why did I miss points on this?"

Don't get me wrong, I do sometimes make errors, and I'm perfectly willing to fix them (e.g., I once typed in an exam score as a 29 instead of a 92). But aside from instructor error, grades are nonnegotiable.

64 Use Faulty Reasoning to Justify Getting the Grade You Want

Students love to invent reasons why they feel they should have gotten a better grade. I have heard all the following faulty reasons and more:

- "I need an A to keep my scholarship."
- "If I fail this class, then won't be able to play on the baseball team."

- "I have to get at least a 'B' in order to keep getting the good student discount on my car insurance."
- "I need to get at least a 'B' to get into the teaching program."
- "If I don't pass this class, my parents will kick me out of the house."

Don't get confused and think these are the *teacher's* problems, they are *your* problems and they are irrelevant to the grade you earned. If you wanted a higher grade you should've studied more effectively, spent more time studying, or both.

Grades are supposed to carry meaning. For instance, if you received an A in a course it means that you exceeded requirements and gave a truly outstanding performance in the course. This is an accomplishment that few students achieve. A C means you met most course requirements and performed satisfactorily in the course. This is the performance level of most students. If your instructor gave all students As, regardless of their performance, then those As would be meaningless.

65 Maintain a "Customer Service" Attitude

As every semester winds down, there are a few phrases that make professors cringe. Here are a few:

- "Can you change my grade to a W? An F will look really bad on my transcripts."
- "Why did you give me such a low grade?"
- "Please call me so we can discuss my grade."
- "Are you going to grade on a curve?"
- "I'm not happy with my grade."

The underlying assumption of these sorts of questions/statements is that you can negotiate your way to a better grade. I kid you not, *as I'm writing this paragraph*, I received a call from Jed, a student who is upset that he received a B this past semester. His exams averaged out at an 86%, he completed most of his homework, so the only item with any wiggle room was his class attendance score. Not surprisingly, Jed wants to discuss his class attendance score. It's important to note that given his other scores, for him to have earned an A in the course he needed to receive 100% on attendance. He received a 75% because he missed five class sessions. Technically, as defined by our college policies, I'm supposed to drop a student from the course for excessive absences after they've missed more than two class sessions. However, because he was otherwise doing well in the course, I didn't drop him. Jed really should have sent me a thank-you note for allowing him to even continue in the class, much less receive a respectable B. Jed seemed to be confusing college with Nordstrom department store. But, unlike Nordstrom, in college there is no customer service center where you can go and exchange your grade for a better one.

If I gave Jed an A, the same grade as my most outstanding students who had consistently high achievement, then my grading policies would lack quality control. A lack of quality control damages our society by turning out students who are not really competent in the subjects in which they are supposed to be competent. It also goes against the behavioral philosophy that serves as the underpinning of my values as a teacher and scientist: we repeat behaviors for which we have been rewarded. I want my students to continue their hard work and achievement, so I reward those behaviors. I don't want students to whine or complain in a vain attempt to make up for a lack of hard work: therefore, those behaviors are ignored.

66 Expect the Most While Giving the Least

I often give students a survey on the first day of class to assess their expectations of the course. On one such survey, I asked students to fill in the blank on the following question: I expect to get a(n)___ in this course. The results were interesting. No one indicated that they expected to receive a D or below, 7% chose a C or better, 58% selected a B or better, and 33% selected an A. Therefore, 91% of the students in that course expected to make at least a B. Less than 33% actually did. It makes me wonder what the weather is like in "fantasy land" where those other 58% of students were living.

Grades are not arbitrary. Teachers don't give out good grades to their favorite students, and grades aren't related to how big you smile or to your good looks. What really matters in the assignment of grades is your *performance* in the class. You will most likely receive the grade you *earned* rather than the grade you *wanted*.

67 Request Extra Credit or Extra, Extra Credit

I engage in a continual ethical struggle regarding extra credit. The problem with extra credit is there is none in life. For example, if you worked for an advertising firm and competed for a big campaign but failed to land it, asking your boss if there is "anything else you could do" for the company to get the commission you would've gotten is futile.

However, sometimes I run across an idea for an assignment that wasn't included in the syllabus and want to give students the opportunity to do it because it's an enriching activity. Therefore, I usually include up to ten points worth of extra credit assignments, which all students have the option of doing. No one is given any extra credit opportunities beyond this, so if you need more extra credit to save your grade in my class, you're out of luck.

It's interesting that as I write this, I'm teaching a summer session class in which I gave students the option of completing an extra credit assignment worth five points that would help them prepare for the midterm. The assignment was due during the same class session as the midterm. Not a single student took me up on the extra credit assignment (which, mind you, was relatively easy). It wasn't because no one was going to need the extra credit: only one student received an A, three got Bs, five got Cs, three got Ds, and ten students got Fs! After the midterm, one student asked if he could do the extra credit, because as it turns out he needs it after all. Nope, too late. And if your professor is nice enough to provide extra credit, and it isn't enough to boost your grade, don't ask for extra, extra credit.

68 Say, "I Don't Understand Why I Got a ___."

"Dr. Cannon, I don't understand why I got a D on the last exam. I studied really hard for it. What should I do?" Hailey asked.

"How many hours did you spend studying for the exam?"

"I spent like four hours studying last night."

"And how many hours did you spend studying before last night?"

"I just read the book before and then studied last night."

"Next time, study for twelve hours and spread it out over several weeks."

"Twelve hours? That's way too much time!"

"Then study four hours and don't worry about the outcome."

If you don't know why you received the grade you did, then you need to ask yourself two questions:

1. **What am I doing that I shouldn't be?** The answer to this first question might be:
   a. Procrastinating
   b. Failing to keep up with the reading
   c. Getting distracted during class
   d. Relying on ineffective study skills (e.g., cramming)

2. What should I be doing that I am not? The answer to this second question might be:
   a. Keeping up with the reading
   b. Actively listening in class and taking notes
   c. Actively reading and taking notes
   d. Spacing your study sessions

Since your professor doesn't live inside your head or even in the same house, he or she cannot possibly guess what you're doing wrong. Only you can figure this out.

I'll admit whenever this situation arises and a student asks me to tell her what she is doing wrong, it irritates me because like Hailey, the student usually doesn't want to find out that more studying is required. If you want to do better without working any harder or smarter, then try one (or all) of the following instead of asking your teacher for advice:

- Wear a lucky charm around your wrist when you take exams.
- Carry a rabbit's foot with you whenever you study.
- Wear your favorite t-shirt inside out during the test.
- Cross your fingers when you hand in an exam.
- Look for and pick up a penny before you take a test.

Or at least realize that your teacher can only help students who really want to help themselves.

69 Ignore the Chain of Command

What exactly is the chain of command in college? Although it varies from school to school, it's usually something like the following:

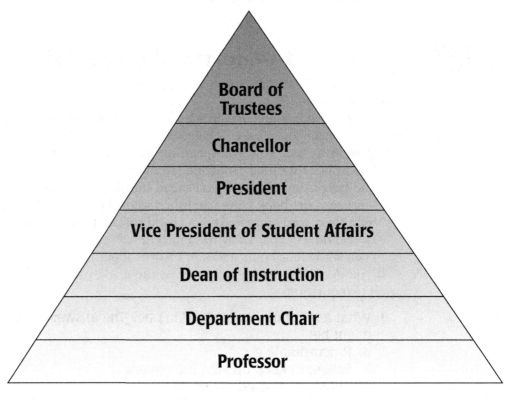

Board of Trustees

Chancellor

President

Vice President of Student Affairs

Dean of Instruction

Department Chair

Professor

FIGURE 6.1

If you have a question or complaint about the topics discussed in class, the techniques used, or in the grading policies, always bring the concern to your teacher first. If you don't give him or her the chance to explain the rules or the reasons behind a policy or technique, you will probably only put your professor on the defensive. If the professor violated policy and doesn't correct his mistake, then you can go to the next person in the chain of command, usually the department chair.

In my class, the policy for final oral presentations is clear: show up on time for your presentation or you will not be allowed to present it and consequently you receive no more than a 50% on the assignment. Why do I have such a strict policy? Simple—when you're late, you're being rude and inconveniencing the other students. No one wants to stop to take the time and explain the game plan for latecomers. I know this for a fact, because when Barbara showed up forty-five minutes late for her presentation, I asked her classmates if the instructions were unclear or unfair. Ninety-five percent of the students agreed that the instructions were clear and fair. Barbara's lab partner even indicated that Barbara reminded her of the "on-time" instructions several days before the presentation!

However, angry that she wasn't allowed to interrupt the rest of the class to present her assignment, and in spite of the policy, Barbara marched straight to the dean's office. The dean, rightly, told her to return to the instructor to discuss the grade. Barbara never returned. Later the dean mentioned that Barbara had stopped by. I explained to her that part of the student's responsibility for the assignment was to listen and respond to other student's presentations and this was clearly spelled out in the instructions for the assignment.

Unfortunately for Barbara, the fact that she went and annoyed the dean annoyed me. If an instructor fails to follow his or her policies, then you might be justified in complaining. But you should never complain to a higher up about a policy that was clear to all and followed to the letter by the instructor. The dean was also annoyed at having her time wasted on such a clear-cut case. It goes without saying that getting everyone annoyed is not the best way to begin an appeal of your grade.

On a couple of occasions, I've had students complain to a dean because the student was unhappy with something I said rather than something I did. In one case, I discussed homosexuality in class. A female student told me she thought it an inappropriate topic for class. If I were a math teacher it would be inappropriate; however, in psychology we discuss topics related to gender and sexuality. The dean agreed with me that the student was wrong. The student was told that although this topic may not be comfortable for her, it was indeed a legitimate topic for a psychology class.

70 Take Your Appeal to the Highest Court

If you go to your teacher with a concern and you're unhappy with the outcome of your conversation, then by all means go to the next person up the chain. But be forewarned: if you're truly in the wrong, appeals can backfire.

I have a story that would be almost hilarious if it weren't so tragic. Back in graduate school when I was teaching for the first time, I taught courses with over 100 students. To make administering exams easier, I proctored exams for a fellow graduate-student teacher named Steven and he proctored exams for me. This way there were always two of us there to pass out exams and discourage wandering eyes.

Imagine my surprise when, in the middle of an exam, one of Steven's students, who I'll call James, pulled out a set of crib notes right in front of me! I did one of those head swivel, "Do my eyes deceive me?" double takes and told Steven what I had just witnessed.

James was caught red-handed with crib notes. Steven and I, being "teaching newbies," proactively went to the department chair's office for advice. The chair said University policy is clear: you can either give James an F on the exam or you can give him an F in the class. The department chair was willing to support whatever decision Steven made.

Steven and I went back to his office to discuss the situation.

I offered my advice, "He is a filthy dirty cheater! Give him an F in the class!" I exclaimed.

Steven was reluctant. "It was his first offense and he was getting a solid B in the class before. I think he should get an F on the exam which will give him a C in the class."

"Who cares how he did before? He is a cheater! Fail him!"

"No, I think I'm leaning towards an F on just that exam."

We were arguing back and forth when James burst into Steven's office. James began swearing and shouting at Steven before Steven could even get a word in.

"I didn't *f&~*k&~^%* cheat!" James shouted.

Steven said, "Excuse me, how can you deny cheating? You had crib notes, which I confiscated and turned into the department chair. The issue isn't whether or not you cheated, it's what to do about it."

Steven and James went back and forth for a while. James was hostile. Steven was calm. I sat there, mouth agape, listening and bearing witness.

"How dare you accuse me of cheating, you *&~^%$!* I'm going to get you!" James shouted so loud that everyone in the nearby offices heard.

Finally after some discussion, Steven told James, "You failed my class!"

"Yeah!" I said.

James almost had a C in the class. Now, he had an F.

It didn't end there. James complained to the department chair. The chair stood by Steven's decision.

Steven and I never heard from James again. However, James went on his own crusade within the university. But, somehow every time James went up the ladder to appeal, he dug himself deeper and deeper into a hole. He barged into the office of the president without an appointment and without knocking. To make a long story short, James ended up on academic probation and was on the verge of being kicked out of the university. I found all this out when I was called by the ombudsman for a statement. The last thing the ombudsman said about James was, "The little bastard will fry."

 TRATEGIES FOR SUCCESSFUL STUDENTS

- Know how to calculate grades and GPAs
- Know minimum GPA requirements for special programs you may be interested in
- Track your scores throughout semester and report clerical errors immediately
- Take responsibility for yourself
- Accept your grades like an adult
- Work extra hard early on, giving yourself a chance to relax later
- Emphasize performance and learning rather than grades
- Discuss concerns with your instructor first

EXERCISE 6.1 *Grades*

1. Wilhemina Tryharder aces all her exams. However she blows off the homework, quizzes, and class participation. Her scores were as follows:

   Exam 1   93/100
   Exam 2   95/100
   Exam 3   90/100
   Exam 4   89/100
   Homework   10/100
   Quizzes   14/100
   Class participation   50/100

   If Wilhemina's teacher grades using a standard scale (i.e., 90% is an A) can she still get an 'A' in the class? If not, what grade will she receive?

2. Norbert Nerdly is taking a class that consists of four exams and an optional final. The instructor drops the lowest exam score. Norbert has taken the first four exams and scored a 70, 72, 69, and 73. There are no other graded assignments in the course. Should Norbert take the final to try and get a better grade in the class? Why or why not?

3. Brauny Noser has just finished his first college semester and his grades in each class are as follows:

Course	Grade	Units
Sociology	B	3
Math	C	3
English	B	3
Biology	C	4
Aerobics	A	1

What is Brauny's GPA?

EXERCISE 6.2   GPA Requirements

Assume you decide to pursue post baccalaureate studies (e.g., graduate school, law school, nursing, teaching credential etc. . .). Choose 5 colleges or universities (not your own) that you might wish to apply to and visit their Web site to find out their minimum GPA requirements for admission to their program.

1. In the chart below, write in the name of each university, the type of program you are interested in, their minimum GPA requirement (for graduate studies in your field), and the URL where you found your information (in case your professor wants to check!):

University	Minimum GPA	Type of Program (e.g., nursing)	URL
1			
2			
3			
4			
5			

2. Next, for one of the programs, call the college or university and find out the actual average GPA of their admitted students last year—that is, the minimum might be a 3.0 to get in but most students applying to that program may have a 3.6!

   a. What did you find out?

   b. How does your own current GPA stack up?

EXERCISE 6.3   Reflection

Please use the following space to reflect on what you've learned from this chapter, and how it can be applied to your life.

CHAPTER 7

Faculty

Flattery: if you want to get to the top, prepare to kiss a lot of the bottom.

—www.despair.com

I was in the bathroom between classes and Judy from my morning class said, "Dr. Cannon, what're *you* doing in here?"

"Umm, probably the same thing you're doing in here."
"Oh, I know *that,* I just meant why are you doing it in *here.*
"Where should I be doing it, the bushes behind the building?"
"Isn't there a teacher's bathroom?"
"Nope. This is it."
"Wow! That's so weird. This is nothing like high school. The teachers there had their own bathrooms."

Judy is right—college isn't like high school, and your college instructors aren't exactly like your high school teachers either. For instance, whereas your high school teachers had college degrees, your college instructors have masters or doctoral degrees. They could've taught children; instead they chose to teach adults, so if you don't currently qualify as an adult you'd better become one quick!

In this chapter you'll learn how college professors are different from high school teachers. Here's a preview:

- Your professors probably won't remind you of due dates or exam dates. They expect you to follow the syllabus and course calendar and be aware of important policies, procedures, and due dates.
- They expect *you* to approach *them* if you're having difficulty. If you're getting an F and haven't come to see them, they will assume it's because you're a flake or you don't care. They won't come to you.
- They are more likely than your high school teachers to have "connections" at universities that can help you. Getting to know them well (especially the professors in your major) can pay off for years to come when you need letters of recommendation or career advice.
- They tend to have more disciplinary power. Whereas a high school teacher can send you to the principal, a college instructor can kick you out of class if you misbehave, so keep your temper and behavior in check.

71 Wait for Your Professor to Come to You

I was a new professor and I made a naïve mistake: almost a third of the semester had passed before I noticed that Curtis had not logged into my course Web site, nor had he completed the mandatory quizzes located there. Thinking that he must not understand the assignment, I approached Curtis.

"Yeah, I know I really need to get cracking on it, I just haven't had time and my computer has been down."

I was a little stunned to find out he had just blown off the assignment and asked, "You're aware that the four quizzes that you missed cannot be made up and they add up to a significant portion of your grade?"

"Yeah, that's why I need to get moving on the current quizzes to improve my grade."

I learned something from interacting with Curtis and others of his ilk: some students can be perfectly aware of assignments, and for whatever reason, simply don't do them. Early in my career, I tried to keep track of which of my 200 students were behind on this or that assignment and offer friendly reminders. Now I maintain my own sanity by waiting for students to come to me if they have concerns about the class or misunderstandings. In the end if they ignore an assignment or due date, it's the student's problem.

Victor was taking a class in which the grade was based on both exams and written assignments. The written assignments consisted of posting messages on a discussion board on the class Web site. This requirement was indicated in the syllabus and spelled out in detail in a separate handout. You needed to post a total of three messages a week on the discussion board; Victor only posted one per week. Without even considering the quality of the content of his messages, he was already earning no more than 33% on this assignment.

Victor earned Bs on all his exams but the F he received for the discussion board assignment brought him down to a C in the class. After noticing his grade for the assignment, Victor asked me, "Why did I get an F on the discussion board? I posted something every week."

"You were required to post *three* messages a week."

"Yeah, but a bunch of people only posted one message per week so I didn't think it would matter."

"It did matter. And anyone else who didn't complete the assignment got Fs, too."

"So why didn't you tell us we needed to post more messages?"

"I *did* tell you. It was in the syllabus and another handout with detailed instructions for completing the assignment."

If you think just because the professor hasn't pulled you aside to ask why you aren't doing your homework or that everything is okay with your performance in the class, think again. Your professor assumes that you're as aware as he or she is as to your standing in the class and that you just don't care.

72 Never Show Appreciation

I used to give out perfect attendance prizes at the end of every semester. This is consistent with my worldview as a behavioral psychologist: don't take good behavior for granted—*reward it.* A few years ago, I stopped this practice. Why? Each term at least one student offended me with rude comments. For example, one semester I gave the perfect attendees an award certificate and a small box of See's candy.

Ethan said, "This candy is crap. This is all I get?"

"What do you mean the candy is crap? That's good quality candy. And what do you mean 'this is all I get'? You also got 100% for attendance and participation. What do your other teachers give you when you get perfect attendance?"

"I don't think I've ever gotten anything before, other than the points."

"Hmm, so maybe you should be grateful that you got something this time."

"Maybe, but I wish I got something better."

Crystal complained, "Can I trade in this prize for some extra credit?"

"You don't get extra credit for perfect attendance; you get a 100% for class participation, and a box of candy because I felt like being nice."

"I'd rather have some more points or some extra credit than this prize."

"Well, I'll think about that idea for next semester."

"That won't help me this semester."

"No, it won't."

"That is so unfair."

"Sorry to change the subject, but what did *you* get *me*?"

"Huh?"

"I was here every day this semester. And did a great job of teaching this class."

"I know. But, that's your job. You have to do that."

"Like showing up and participating is your job, right?"

"I guess."

"So where is my prize, my certificate, or my token of appreciation?"

"Umm . . ."

In fact, this is a perfect example of another behavioral principle: punish a good behavior and it declines in frequency. Here, by punishing the teacher's reward-giving behavior, her reward-giving behavior diminished.

I had a choice: either give those students who did what they were expected to do—attend every class—some acknowledgement to say that I noticed or appreciated, or I could do nothing at all (beyond assigning the appropriate participation score). I decided that next time I'll do nothing at all. In essence, my reward-giving behavior was eliminated by ungrateful comments from students. Unfortunately, the many students who were grateful and gracious will also be ignored.

It's possible my experiences are distorted by living in "the OC" (Orange County, California) where the average home is priced at over half a million dollars—"give-me" attitudes are probably more likely here. To me, with a gift, it's the thought that counts, not the price tag.

In contrast, I can count on one hand the number of times each year that my own hard work gets acknowledged by students. One or two students will write a nice thank-you note or give me a small gift. Since I teach about 500 students a year, this means I'm formally thanked by less than 1% of students.

I'm not making a plea for cards and gifts from my students; I don't do what I do just for praise. However, it would be nice to get a written thank you note for "going the extra mile" when I write last-minute letters of recommendation or agree to serve as a reference for students who are applying for off-campus jobs. I don't have to do these favors, but I do.

73 Don't Learn Names

Last semester, Jenny called me by a different name every day. "Dr. Condor, I have a question" or "Excuse me, Dr. Kanner, is this on the study guide?" and so forth.

There is only one of me—how hard can it be to remember my name? In that particular class, there were thirty students and I knew all of their names—even Jenny's. How can you go through three or four months of instruction without even learning your instructor's name?

My name is not a secret. On the first meeting day of every class, I tell students they have two choices:

1. call me Dr. Cannon or
2. call me Cari.

I explicitly tell them that I don't respond to "Miss" (I'm a grown woman) "Mrs." (my husband has a different last name than me) or "Ms." (because I earned a Ph.D.). Still, I'm addressed as "Mrs. Cannon" or "Ms. Cannon" (one student even called me "Mr. Cannon")!

I'm frequently mistaken for a student or teaching assistant. My advice is that if all else fails, err on the side of flattery by calling the instructor "Professor"; either you'll be correct or, if the teacher hasn't yet earned that title, it's still flattering.

74 Try to Become Your Professor's Best Friend

If there were such a thing as "frequent office-hour miles," Melanie would have earned a trip around the world. She came in to my office every day, plopped down her bag and made herself comfortable. She didn't ask too many class-related questions, so mostly we just chatted.

I enjoy chatting with students and getting to know them better. Yet it's a little like any other relationship in that compatibility is an issue, and Melanie and I did not have compatible personalities. In all honesty, we had a major personality clash! Anyone could see it—anyone, that is, except Melanie. She invited me out to lunch, parties, church, the park, and the mall. Each time I said a polite "no, thanks." Melanie was a good student and I would have been happy to spend time assisting her with her coursework or writing a letter of recommendation but I'd never want to go on a cruise with her. She was a bit histrionic, frequently shouting in public places, and always drawing attention to herself, while I'm much more reserved.

I hate to say this, in case Melanie is listening, but I do sometimes become "friends" with former students. When I say friends, I don't mean that I hang out with them often, share intimate secrets, and go on trips together; it's a bit more of a mentorship than a true friendship. In every case, the student is exceptional and well-suited to my personality—the kind of person I could have become friends with regardless of how I met him or her. I won't apologize to Melanie, or anyone else, for my preferences anymore than I could apologize for falling in love with my husband. Some people click, some people don't.

If your instincts about people are sometimes off, it's best to assume that your teacher does not want to become your closest friend and keep your interactions professional.

75 Hit on Your Professor

College professors are often a motley bunch: some of us are so ill-groomed and poorly dressed we could pass for street urchins. But if you're one of the lucky few to have a teacher that's easy on the eyes, please don't embarrass yourself by asking him or her out (especially if he or she is married!).

I speak from experience. RJ was an intellectually bright but socially inept student. It sort of amazed me how he could breeze through organic chemistry and mechanical physics and not be able to get a "read" on people. Perhaps it shouldn't have come as such a shock when he apparently wondered if we had some "chemistry" going on ourselves! He followed me around with "puppy dog" eyes, and somehow managed to ignore my painful cringing, downward glances, and rapid terminations of conversations that should've indicated that his attentions weren't welcome.

At RJ's graduation, he gave me a gift and suggested that I open it later. When I opened it, I found out why he didn't want to be there—it was a ceramic candle holder with an "I'm hot for you" inscription on it. I think it burned my fingers and the candle wasn't even lit. *Yuck!* Was he for real?

I showed the gift to my husband and said, "Do you want to kick his butt?"

"I'm a little mad," he said, "but I actually feel more pity than anger. I wouldn't have done something that pathetic to tell a girl I liked her even when I was twelve years old."

"So you can feel my pain?"

"Oh yeah."

I have known single teachers and students who have dated, usually after the semester is over. In every case it has ended badly, and almost always the student gets the worst of it.

Needless to say, if your instructor is single and attractive and you're wondering whether he or she is interested, keep wondering until the semester is over. If your instructor is attractive and *married,* keep your romantic thoughts to yourself.

76 Say, "You Aren't Being Fair!"

Or at least, don't say, "You aren't being fair" when what you really mean is, "This sucks!" What's the difference? First, let's define "fair." Strictly speaking, fairness implies that all students had the same opportunities to succeed, received unbiased assessments, and there was no favoritism of one student over another. It also means applying the rules equally to everyone.

Most students who complain about fairness are talking about a score on an assessment (e.g., project, quiz, or paper) or their final grade. When questioned, students typically admit that the grade they received is indeed the grade they earned; they just *aren't happy about it.*

Can teachers be unfair? Sure, if your teacher springs a term paper assignment on you in the last one-fourth of the semester when it wasn't listed in the syllabus, that's unfair. Why? The teacher didn't play by his or her own rules as put forth in the syllabus. But if you've flubbed or failed to turn in major assignments and you think you're still entitled to a good grade, you're deluded. College is preparation for life, and if you miss a deadline on a major assignment in your job, start polishing your resúme.

77 Never Use Office Hours

Years ago when I was a graduate student and teaching for the first time, I received some bad news: a friend had become terminally ill. This was a stressful time in my life, and this announcement was the last straw. As I sat outside the department discussing the problem with a friend, I began to cry. Undeterred by my tears, Libby (a student in one of my courses) approached.

"I need to talk to you about my grade in your class."

"Now is not a good time," I sobbed, "please come by during office hours."

"I can't, I have a class then. I really need to speak to you *now*."

"I can't . . . (sob) . . . talk . . . (sob) . . . now. I'm . . . (sob) . . . busy."

"I insist on speaking to you NOW."

My friend said, "Can't you see we are having a serious conversation? It isn't her office hours and you're making a nuisance of yourself. Go away."

At any other professional's office, you would never just show up and expect to be seen on the spot. Can you imagine a newly hired junior executive barging into the CEO's office and demanding to be seen without an appointment?

Why do students assume that if they've "caught you" they can insist on service on the spot? I've had students attempt to discuss their grade at the gym, the mall, a restaurant, even the bathroom. Being approached anywhere and everywhere is a little like the medical doctor who has neighbors ask them for free medical advice at cocktail parties ("Does this look infected to you?").

The reason that this on-the-spot behavior is so annoying is that I keep five office hours each week where I sit in my office waiting for students to visit. The irony is that 99% of the time, no one shows up.

Students who show up to office hours once or twice almost always become frequent users of this service. Why? They discover that cool things happen:

- You get to visit with your professor in a more relaxed atmosphere than the classroom and discover the real person behind all the glamour (hah!).
- You might get study tips or hints on exams.
- You can get inside information on getting into particular schools.
- You can get career advice.

Find out your professor's office hours and take advantage of them.

78 Be Invisible

Avoiding office hours is not enough—try to be as forgettable as possible. Make sure you never stand out in class by answering questions or volunteering for demonstrations.

Desiree had recently graduated from college and wanted to pursue a graduate degree in psychology, so she emailed me recently to see if I could get her into one of my alma maters. Unfortunately, I had no idea who she was! I'm sorry, but I can't make a phone call on behalf of someone I don't even know.

Conversely, there are some students who I will never forget. They could call me today—even though I haven't seen them in five years—ask me for a favor, and I'm happy to oblige if I can. To be sure this happens in your case, make yourself memorable by speaking up in class or stopping by during office hours. Otherwise, don't be sorry if your professor can't recognize you after a few semesters have gone by. Take every class with the expectation that you may need a letter of recommendation from that teacher in the future.

On the first day of class, I sometimes ask students to tell me a little about themselves. Most mention (usually somewhat sheepishly) that their major is undecided, undeclared, or unknown. That's okay—it isn't important to pick your major right away, so go ahead and take a number of different classes to decide where your interests lie. However, even if you haven't decided what you will eventually do with your life, you're already laying the foundation for your entire professional future. If you assume that just because your major is undecided you will never need current faculty again after the semester ends, then you're doing yourself an incredible disservice.

Faculty will ultimately become your single biggest career resource because:

- They have connections with their former graduate school buddies who are now teaching at colleges and universities all over the country.
- They serve on scholarship and valedictorian committees for your college.
- They are the most credible individuals to write letters of recommendation or serve as character references for you.

I have had some interesting visits, phone calls, and emails from former students. They usually begin with "I'm not sure you remember me, but . . ." and have finished with such gems as, "I'm applying to your alma mater and was hoping you'd put in a good word for me," to "I'm being prosecuted for statutory rape and was hoping you'd serve as a character witness for me." If you never took the time to get to know me when you were taking my class, then I'm not going to be willing or able to be of much help.

79 Complain, Criticize, and Whine

Every night as class was starting Derek would ask:

"Are you going to keep us the whole time?"

"Probably."

"Why can't we leave early, just this once?"

"Give me a break. You're the one who signed up for a three-hour class. Why did you sign up if you can't handle it?"

"I didn't think we'd really be here for three hours."

Each night when class was underway, Derek would noticeably yawn or turn to look at the clock. He'd make occasional "suggestions" such as: "a few more jokes would help," or "tell us another funny story." He purposely made these comments to be contrary. My lectures are far from boring—there are plenty of jokes and stories (sometimes more colorful than you bargained for).

What I remember most fondly about Derek was the day that he got up to do his oral presentation. His public speaking debut was a total failure. He stuttered, said "um" dozens of times, and more than once he actually begged the audience for help. In a nutshell, he stank! A future orator he was not. Neither the other students nor myself, said anything critical. We nodded. We smiled. We forgave his debacle. We let him retain some of his dignity (well as much dignity as a guy with four nipple piercings can have).

The experience changed Derek. He suddenly stopped whining and needling me. Life on the other side of the podium had apparently taught him something about my role in the classroom.

If you want to be a "Derek" there are lots of things you can complain about including the:

- Length of the class
- Difficulty of the material
- Lack of obvious and/or immediate practicality of the material
- Excess homework
- Strict grading policies

Whining about these things is not going to change them. The class will still be three hours long, and you still need to learn the material even if you think you aren't ever going to need it.

Very few of your professor's choices about what to cover are arbitrary. They've carefully selected the material that they teach in order to prepare you to advance to the next course. For instance, every time I teach *Research Methods in Psychology,* I hear a bit of whining about all the papers that have to be written and the level of effort that must go into writing them.

Unlike those students who whine, I have seen beyond the *Methods* class into the future. I know what these students will be in for as upper division psychology majors because I've taught upper division courses. When my students see how well I have prepared them to compete with the students in their future courses, they'll thank me.

80 Overestimate Your Professor's Concern for You

As faculty we are concerned about our students, but *our concern is an exponentially decreasing function over time.* For those of you who don't understand "math speak," this means we care a great deal about you during the first weeks of class but our concern decreases sharply over the course of the semester; by the time we turn in grades, you are no longer in our thoughts. Let me illustrate using two students: Brenda and Dylan.

On Monday of the second week of the semester, Brenda came up after class and said, "Dr. Cannon, I took the first quiz and when I tried to submit it, it showed up as incomplete in my grades list."

"Let's take a look and see if the quiz score got posted to my grade-book." It hadn't so we problem solved until we found out what Brenda had done wrong and in less than five minutes the problem was fixed. Had it taken half an hour I'd have still been happy to help Brenda.

On the other hand, Dylan came up to me on the last day of class and said, "For some reason, none of my quiz scores were posted to my grades list."

"What? Why did you wait until now to say something? It's too late to do anything about it now."

"I really did all the quizzes, I don't want to lose points for them."

"You waited until all forty-five quizzes were over to say something? Now you want me to 'trust you' that you did them? Unfortunately, it doesn't work that way."

I'll admit that during the last two to three weeks of the semester I'll intentionally hide from students because I don't care anymore if you are unhappy with your grade or that you don't understand why you did so poorly—and I don't even want to hear about it. Eight or ten weeks ago, I'd have explained the material over and over until you understood it or helped you solve a problem you were having in the course. Now, I am already planning for next semester's students.

81 Don't Cultivate Mentors

Kelly was a psychology major who'd earned an A in two of my classes. She was now taking her third class with me and had meant to talk to me about careers in psychology, but she was shy so she'd put it off. This semester she finally stopped by during office hours to ask a few questions. I happily provided the answers and suggested she return after reading some resources I'd recommended. So far, she hasn't returned. To shy students like Kelly, professors are intimidating.

If you are a good student, but intimidated by professors, then you probably don't take advantage of their knowledge and experience after you leave the classroom. If so, you may be missing out on some great opportunities. Outside of the classroom, professors serve as mentors, providing inside knowledge on careers in their fields and helping you gain valuable experience.

The trick is finding a good match between yourself and a possible mentor. Your professor might consider you as a "mentee" if you:

- Received high grades from him or her
- Had excellent attendance and class participation
- Showed interest and initiative outside of the classroom
- Have compatible interests and personalities

Your professor may be a possible mentor if he or she is:

- Energetic and passionate about what is taught in the classroom
- Enjoys interacting with students outside the classroom (e.g., serves as a club advisor or coach of some sort)
- Actively involved in college activities (e.g., serves on committees or coordinates events and doesn't just teach class and go home)

When there is a good match between teacher and student, then great things can happen for the student such as:

- Gaining experience as a teaching assistant
- Earning credit for independent study

- Access to awards and scholarships associated with professional organizations of which your professor is a member
- Letters of recommendation
- Internships

If you are one of the lucky few students who receive mentoring from a professor, then treat this as the privilege that it is and remember to thank the professor appropriately

82 Ask for Recommendation Letters the Wrong Way

"Dr. Cannon, can I ask a favor?" begins Navid.

"What's that?" I ask.

"I'm applying for an internship and I need a letter of recommendation. The application is due in two days."

"TWO DAYS? I'd love to help you Navid, but I can't write a letter for you in two days. First, because I already have commitments this week, and second, I've only known you for a little over a month!"

"Please! I don't really know any other professors well, and I'm desperate. Can't you just write up something?"

"The best I could write is something that says, 'Navid is in my Child Psychology course and has earned a solid B during the first month of the semester. He seems bright and capable. Please give him your utmost consideration.'"

"That would be great! Can you do that?" begs Navid.

"Okay. I'm not sure it will help, but that is all I know about you, and can say firsthand."

If Navid was applying for a competitive internship, scholarship, or as is often the case when students ask for a letter, to graduate school, then the letter I wrote for him *might be worse than no letter at all.* This is because other students have letters that say, 'John has been my research assistant for two years. He helped run studies with mice, analyzed data, and has co-authored two papers with me,' or 'Jane was the president of the Anthropology Club. She organized a fundraiser and used the funds to bring a world-renowned primatologist as a speaker to our campus. This wouldn't have happened without Jane's initiative.' Some of the letters for these top-notch students are 3 pages long and include detailed descriptions and firsthand observations. A letter like Navid's lets the committee reviewing applications know that he didn't take the initiative to get to know faculty well. And they'll assume he'll be just as apathetic in the future.

If you need a recommendation letter, please do the following.

- Only ask faculty who know you really well and can write a *strong* letter. It's best if you've taken the instructor for two or more courses, or you've worked with him outside the classroom for some time (e.g., sports team, club member, teaching assistant). If a professor says no, don't beg, or this will be reflected in the letter.
- Ask at least one month in advance.
- Ask in person (unless you live in another time zone) rather than by mail or e-mail.
- Come prepared with a personal statement, resume, and all relevant forms and instructions.
- Follow up with a written thank you note.

83 Ignore Proper E-tiquette

These days, very few students call me and even fewer physically show up to office hours. Outside of the classroom, most of the communication I have with students is via e-mail. It's easy and convenient for students and professors (except the "traditional" ones who don't wish to change) alike and so I can appreciate students' reliance on it. However, e-mail makes it easier for students to at best leave a bad impression and at worst really tick off the instructor. Let me give you an example of an e-mail I received last summer:

> *dear sir:*
>
> *I wish to take your online psychology class but before I do, can you send me a syllabus? Also I've never taken an online class before so if you could tell me how the course operates, how much work we do, and when we meet ect.*
>
> *Thanks,*
> *Lost in Cyberspace*

Before you read any further, what did Lost in Cyberspace do wrong? Where do I begin? He doesn't know my name (or gender). He has spelling and grammatical errors—the older the professor, the more this is going to irritate them. As a Gen-Xer this doesn't bother me as much as it does my Baby Boomer colleagues; I can "lol" and "btw" with the best of 'em. The tone of his e-mail is demanding and by his own admission he appears ignorant of the skills needed for success in an online class.

Does Lost in Cyberspace think I'm going to send him an essay outlining the course procedures? The reason this is irritating is you wouldn't show up to a classroom 2 weeks before school started and complain that you couldn't get access to the instructor or course materials. So why does it seem reasonable to e-mail me during summer vacation and demand a syllabus that I might not have finished until the day class begins? I was too annoyed to think up something polite, and I knew from experience that if I replied, Lost in Cyberspace would have at least two follow-up e-mails. So I didn't reply to Lost in Cyberspace or the other 100+ students with similar requests. If I answered all of these e-mails I'd have to give up my summer vacation!

I've received so many weird, raunchy, whiny, emails that I might have to write another book. I've been forwarded chain letters, prayers, naughty jokes, and once I got a rather long letter about how I was going to hell when I died. Most of these annoying emails can be categorized as head scratchers, head slappers, gut clenchers, or foot stompers:

Head scratchers (I didn't get enough information to answer your question).

> Example: "I missed class and don't want to fall behind. What chapter are we reading in class this week?" From: punkazkid@myschoolsmail.com.
> I don't know who she is or what class she's in!

Head slappers (or TMI—too much information!).

> Example: "Just wanted to let you know I won't be in class today. I have a really bad case of diarrhea and can't get off the toilet for more than a minute." From: got2run@bigu.edu. Did he really tell me that?

Gut clenchers (I'm laughing at your expense).

> Example: "I am in your online Introduction to Psychology course, but I can't seem to find out which room it's in." From: cluelessinseattle@somecollege.edu. Believe it or not, I get this one every semester.

Foot stompers (Now I'm mad!).

> Example: "I sent you an email an hour ago and you still haven't responded! You obviously aren't concerned with your students." From: mememe@universityofme.edu

When you e-mail your instructors, please make sure your message is similar to one you'd write as a businessperson—that is, colleague to colleague rather than one you'd send to a friend. Remember to follow proper etiquette which includes:

- Spell your professor's name correctly.
- Include relevant information like your first and last name and the course/section you are in.
- Include a clear subject that states your purpose for the e-mail. For instance: don't use, "hi" instead use, "question about chapter 03 homework in biopsych."
- Don't add your professors to mass e-mailings, and don't forward funny pictures, stories, or other junk. They get enough of that crud from their own friends.
- Keep the message simple and concise, watch the tone of your message, and avoid emotional language.
- Discuss emotional issues face-to-face rather than via e-mail.
- Remember that e-mail is not always private.
- Don't ask your instructor to write an essay.
- Check your spelling, grammar, and punctuation.
- Don't SCREAM (i.e., write in all caps) or use fancy backgrounds or fonts.
- Don't ask for confidential information (grades) via e-mail.

STRATEGIES FOR SUCCESSFUL STUDENTS

- Behave maturely, professionally, and treat faculty respectfully even when you're angry or frustrated
- Let your professor know if you appreciated his/her class or teaching style
- Attend office hours or make an appointment
- Come prepared: bring thoughtful questions
- When interacting with faculty, you can keep it friendly, without becoming intimate friends
- Try to be visible enough to be memorable (in a positive way)
- Remember that one day, your professor may be able to help you with a letter of recommendation or on an awards committee

EXERCISE 7.1 *Faculty*

So far in college, which professors have you appreciated the most? Explain.

What type of teaching style do you benefit from the most (e.g., lecture, small group discussion)? Why?

List the office hours and office locations of your current professors.

Where did your current professors get their degrees? (Hint: most college catalogs list the names of full-time faculty and their degree institutions).

Now is your chance to get even. What are your biggest pet peeves about your professors?

EXERCISE 7.2 Asking for Letters of Recommendation from Faculty

Assume that you are applying for a scholarship, entrance to graduate school, and/or a job, and you are about to ask a faculty member for a letter of recommendation. You'll need to present your professor with a detailed resume, so he or she can write an informed letter. Use the prompts below to organize your thoughts and information:

Before you ask your professor:

1. Are you asking a professor who knows you well enough to write a good letter? Remember, you don't need *any* letter, you need a *good* letter.

2. Are you asking the professor at least 1 month in advance of the due date?

After you've asked your professor (and he/she has said yes), you'll need to provide the following information:

3. What type of scholarship/degree/job are you seeking?

4. What are your goals in seeking the scholarship/degree/job?

5. Does your resume include the following?
    a. GPA

    b. Relevant courses taken

    c. Relevant work experience

    d. Relevant volunteer work

    e. Awards and honors received

    f. Professional memberships and activities

6. Did you let the professor know when the due date is?

7. Did you provide the professor with all appropriate forms and a postage-paid envelope?

8. Did you follow up with a thank you?

EXERCISE 7.3   Reflection

Please use the following space to reflect on what you've learned from this chapter, and how it can be applied to your life.

Educational and Career Planning

> **Planning: much work remains to be done before we announce our total failure to make any progress.**
>
> *—www.despair.com*

A wise friend of mine once said, "All jobs involve dealing with crap—the trick is to find a job where the crappy parts don't bother you." For instance, in customer service jobs you sometimes have to deal with unhappy customers, but if you enjoy working with people maybe you don't mind this aspect of your work. In my friend's case, however, she meant it quite literally—she cleaned up pigeon poop in a laboratory. Cleaning poop wasn't the main part of her job, she was a scientist who studied pigeon behavior, but it was the crappy part.

As I was completing my postdoctoral internship and researching potential jobs, I realized I needed to follow my friend's advice: find a career I loved doing, one in which I didn't mind the worst parts of the job. It seemed simple enough, but looking back, choosing a career was not easy. There I was, Ph.D. already in hand, and I was *still* trying to figure out exactly what I wanted to be when I grew up. I knew that I was passionate about psychology, but what did I want to do with it every day: conduct research, consult, or teach?

At first I considered conducting research. It was, after all what I'd been trained to do. On some level, research is exciting and glamorous—you are at the forefront of knowledge and discovery and jobs at major research universities are highly prestigious. But watching rats press levers in the laboratory just didn't rock my world.

Next I considered consulting in business and industry. I knew that using behavioral psychology to solve performance problems in companies would be fun, but what else would such a job entail? In the course of my planning and research, I cultivated a contact who was an executive at a consulting firm. I was considering a job similar to hers and wanted to ask her what it was like. She was nice enough to spend some time discussing her field with me. In the middle of one of our telephone conversations she stopped and said, "I really need to get off the phone. I've to catch a plane to Chicago in a few hours. Can you call me back? Let's see—when will I be home? Today is Tuesday, Thursday I'm going to Miami so that won't work, then Friday I head to Seattle, and I'll be home Sunday. Can you call me Sunday? I'll be leaving again Monday for Atlanta so Sunday might work best."

Later, thinking about that phone conversation made me realize that I didn't want to work for a company that had you jetting all over the country every few days. Occasional travel is fun, but constantly moving around and living out of a suitcase is exhausting. That just wasn't the lifestyle for me, which meant consulting was out. Imagine if I had never conducted research on consulting jobs: if I just accepted one, I would have been miserable.

The answer to my job search woes came to me one day when I walked from my lab (where I had been frustrated all day by trying to solve an equipment problem) and into my classroom to teach. In the middle of a lecture, as I looked out at my students, I thought: I love *this*. I'd been teaching only one day a week and realized teaching was what I should be doing *every day*.

As you plan your own major and career, allow me to insist on one thing: when picking a career, pick one that'll allow you to look forward to Mondays. If on Sunday night you're anxious because you have to go to work tomorrow, then you're in the wrong profession. But whatever you do, begin planning now.

Maybe it seems too difficult to do all the planning and research that it will take to choose a career wisely; maybe you'd rather just sit back and wait for a career to choose you. If you do, be forewarned, this will ensure a lifetime of anxiety-filled Sundays.

84 Assume It's No Big Deal to Drop and Retake Classes

A few minutes before class started, I overheard a conversation between a couple of students.

Dan said, "I was failing my pre-algebra class, so I dropped it. I'm going to retake it next semester so I can do better."

Mary followed with, "Oh, I hate math! I took pre-algebra last semester and I didn't get it at all. I did so bad I couldn't bear to take it this semester, so I'm going to take it next semester, too. Maybe we'll be in there together."

Here's the reality: most students fail their first math class, retake it, and fail it again (and again!). The probability is that both Dan and Mary will be in pre-algebra twice more. Statistically speaking, they will also fail twice more and never get to the next course in the math sequence.

At the college where I teach, the research department conducted a study of students' progress through the math sequence. They looked at three years' worth of pass rates. They discovered that less than half (roughly 40%) of students who attempted a math class successfully completed it. Of the 60% who failed their first semester and retook math the following semester, only about 9% of those students passed on the second or even third attempt.

Why do students keep failing? My own casual observation of students who've retaken my courses suggests it's because they make the same mistakes over and over again. They assume that classes are like the lottery—the more you play the more likely you'll win. But winning at math (or any other subject) doesn't involve luck; it involves keeping up with daily assignments and mastering material before moving on. So students keep signing up for the same class semester after semester, but they don't make the necessary behavioral changes to be successful.

Byron made the same mistake three times in my class. I first met Byron in the spring semester. He started out okay, but by the middle of the semester his attendance became spotty and he carelessly missed an exam. When I threatened to drop him for excessive absences, he swore he would improve his attendance and pull up his grade. I was skeptical. He ended up failing the class.

In the fall semester he was back. I asked him, "Are you going to be serious this time, Byron?"

"Yes! I ran into some personal problems last semester and it won't happen again. I don't want to have to repeat this class a third time."

"Great, I hope you pass this time because, and no offense, I don't want to see you in this class again!"

"You won't!"

Once again Byron started out doing well, but mid-semester he started missing a lot of classes. Then, as you can guess, he managed to miss an exam and eventually dropped the class again.

He was back the *following* spring semester—and did exactly the same thing (the first time he missed a class, I fantasized about going into his house and pouring cold water all over him to wake him up). Unfortunately, Byron faded away that semester yet again. Sadly, there are lots of Byrons.

85 Say, "My Counselor Wasn't Helpful"

"My counselor screwed up big time," Glenda complained, "he told me to take *Physical Anthropology* and I don't even need it. I should have taken *Cultural Anthropology* instead."

"Really? That's odd. Are you transferring to some place we don't articulate with?"

"No, I'm just going to Fullerton."

"That's really weird, because we transfer many students there. There shouldn't be any mistakes. *Most* of our students go there, so the counselors must really know those requirements."

"I know. I didn't really want to go there. I wanted to go to San Diego but I can't afford to move out. This way I can stay with my parents and save some money."

"You were going to go to San Diego? Did you talk to your counselor and get the information about requirements for admission to San Diego?"

"Yes."

"And then you changed your mind and decided to go to Fullerton?"

"Yes."

"I'll bet your counselor didn't give you erroneous information. He gave you accurate information for transfer to San Diego and then you changed your mind and the requirements are different for Fullerton."

"Maybe you're right."

There is no universal curriculum. If you change your major, or decide to change to a different college, then you'll have taken classes you *don't* need, and you'll need to take additional classes that you *do* need. To make matters worse, the requirements change every year (see the catalog for the year you begin).

The counselors at your institution give you the most up-to-date information they have. However, you need to see them early in your college career and continue to see them each semester to continue getting the most current information. Even if you think you can read college articulation plans yourself, it's still very helpful to visit the counseling office. Counselors provide a number of services. These include helping students:

- Plan a course of study
- Understand graduation requirements
- Learn about transfer options, baccalaureate, and graduate degrees
- If you plan to transfer from a 2- to 4-year college prepare for a career

Counselors are up to date on trends and tips for transferring to four-year institutions. They know which college admissions reps are most helpful, and they can tell you about courses that aren't required but which can make you more competitive. They arrange college fairs on campus where you can meet reps or sign up for university tours. A stop at the counseling center now can save you time and headaches in the future.

The counselors who specialize in career planning can also help you realistically evaluate your abilities, interests, talents, and personality characteristics in order to develop appropriate academic and career goals. However, none of the services offered by the counseling staff will be helpful to you unless you go into each meeting with specific questions and leave prepared to do additional research on your own.

86 Don't Read the **College Catalog**

"Hi, Joy! How was your summer?"

"It was really nice. How was yours, Dr. Cannon? Did you get to relax some?"

"Yes, I got in a little free time and feel refreshed."

"You'll be seeing a lot of me this semester. I'm taking three of your courses."

"Wow, I guess I should be flattered," I laughed.

"I really enjoyed your *Intro* class last semester, but I figured I might as well get a bunch of psych classes out of the way since I've decided to major in psychology."

"You don't need to take *all* of the psych classes here to be a psych major. Most schools require only two to three to enter the upper division classes when you transfer."

"I also want to get an AA degree in psychology along the way, though."

"We only require three classes including *Intro,* which you already took, and *Research Methods,* which you didn't sign up for."

"Oh. Maybe I should have taken that class instead."

"Of course you're welcome to take my other courses as electives, but you probably have many other requirements to fulfill: math, English, history and such."

"How are you supposed to know what to take, then?"

"It's in the *College Catalog.*"

"I didn't see it in there. I just saw the classes listed for this semester."

"That wasn't the catalog. That was the *Schedule of Classes.*"

"What's the difference?"

"I think you need to get a copy of the catalog and find out."

Most students have looked at the *Schedule of Classes.* It lists the classes offered during the current semester along with times, meeting dates, and room numbers. However, many students have never read the most important publication on campus—the *College Catalog.* Or, like Joy, they don't realize the difference between the catalog and the *Schedule of Classes.* The catalog is the most important tool for understanding the policies of the college and the courses offered. The catalog contains a wealth of information including:

- A list of college majors and degree programs
- Policies
- Prerequisites

- The academic calendar with important dates (e.g., drop dates and holidays)
- A list of available student services
- Information on receiving credit by exam or other means, sources of financial aid and requirements for receiving honors at graduation.

Students frequently mention that they plan to take a particular course with me in the upcoming spring only to be surprised to find out it's only offered in the fall. If you ignore the catalog, you may waste time taking the wrong classes or mistakenly plan to take a course during a semester it isn't offered. In the end it may not matter as long as you don't mind taking classes on the ten-year plan.

87 Don't Make Short- and Long-Term Goals

On the first day of class I asked several students to tell me why they were taking the class.

John said, "I need it to transfer."

Bob said, "For general education requirements."

Lindsey said, "It fit into my schedule."

Very few students have really thought about the courses they are taking; sometimes they have no idea whether the course is required or even transferable. They simply may've heard good things about the instructor or the meeting time fit conveniently into their schedule.

Even if you don't have a plan for where you'd like to end up in the future, you'll still end up somewhere. Without a plan, you may not like where you end up. Have you ever been to a party where all your twenty-something friends are having a great time and a thirty-year-old guy walks in and does his best to act cool, hitting on all the nineteen-year-old girls and making everyone cringe? I remember being eighteen or nineteen and looking at my friends and saying, "He doesn't even have a clue! He should have a career, a wife, and a house or something."

Well, let's step into the thirty-year-old's mind for a moment. He used to be twenty-one and cool. Sure, he partied, but he had his whole future to look forward to. But then everyone else his age wrapped up their college education and moved on. He didn't notice, but somehow, the years just slipped away. He feels the same on the inside. What happened?

Trust me when I say that after twenty-one, time just starts flying by, so that the older you get the faster time seems to pass. You feel the same on the inside so you're shocked when someone says to you, "You're *so* out of touch." Wait a minute, I was so cool a couple of years ago!

Like the older guy at the party, whether or not you go to college, you age. Where do you want to be when you're thirty, forty, or fifty? Everyone has goals. Yet not everyone takes the time to sit and reflect on their goals, write them down, or to determine if their short and long term goals are in conflict. For instance, you may have a goal of making a lot of money, meeting new people, or having fun. To reach the goal of making a lot of money in the future, you usually have to give up a little fun in the present (e.g., by studying and not partying) for a big payoff in the future (e.g., getting a degree and then a high paying full time job).

If you don't write down your goals now, then don't complain if you hate where you are at thirty-, forty-, or fifty-years old.

88 Assume the Right Career Will Fall from the Sky

Sandy came to my office and we discussed her future.

"I've been here for three years and I still haven't picked a major," Sandy complained.

"What are your career goals?" I asked.

"That's the problem, I don't know yet."

"I'm not asking what you want to do *exactly*, just what do you need in a career to make you happy?"

"What do you mean?"

"Well, other than complaining to me, what are you doing to try and find out what would make you happy? Have you been analyzing your skills or interests?"

"Not really. I guess I've just been thinking about it a lot."

"Your first stop should be the career center to explore your skills, interests, and values."

"Maybe I'll do that if I can find some time."

Students seem to think that one day, just by accident, a job title will fall from the sky and suddenly they'll have an epiphany: "That's it! I'm going to be a chicken puller!"* The point is that many people do jobs that cannot be captured with a specific job title. Their job, if they are lucky, captures a combination of their strengths and interests. To land your dream job, you will need to do a *lot* of research.

*What's a chicken puller? It's someone who removes the guts from a chicken before it goes to market.

89 Choose an Unrealistic Career Goal

I recently asked one of my students, a psych major named Robbie, what he wanted to be when he grew up.

"I'm going to be a college professor," he answered.

This struck me as odd because Robbie was extremely shy and quiet. In one of my classes, he gave the required in-class oral presentation while looking so uncomfortable you'd think his underwear was three sizes too small. He spoke with awkward pauses and a liberal amount of "Ums." Besides, Robbie was academically mediocre. So I asked him:

"What made you want to become a professor?"

His response was a nonchalant shrug and a "It just seemed like it would be cool to have the summers off."

I explained to Robbie that the competition to become a college professor is so stiff that he should only consider it as a career if he:

1. Is ultra competitive with good grades, superior standardized test scores, and participation in extra curricular activities like research.
2. Can *only* see himself as a professor, because after obtaining his doctorate he will likely spend ten years or more unemployed or underemployed waiting for a full-time job (this is often true of even very well prepared and competent individuals).

Chances are, Robbie will never be a college professor. If he did a little informational interviewing with a few college faculty members, he'd likely learn this really quickly. If you prepare for a career that doesn't match up with your skills, values, and interests, you'll be making a huge mistake.

90 Postpone Researching Future Jobs

I met Lynnette when we both volunteered to serve as mentors in a summer program for undergraduates interested in science careers. The program was designed to lure students from the more popular practical sciences (e.g., medicine) into more basic sciences (i.e., research). Ironically, the volunteers, who were graduate and postdoctoral students in the sciences, were supposed to encourage students to choose careers as bench scientists, while they themselves, trained as bench scientists, were being drawn toward careers as teachers and practitioners.

Lynnette was about two-thirds of the way finished with her doctorate in particle physics. When I met her, she was already an accomplished physicist. She had published several important scientific articles in her field and received several awards for her research. There was only one problem: Lynnette was miserable. After all her hard work and science training, Lynnette realized that she didn't enjoy working in a laboratory. She felt detached from her true passion: sharing her love of science with children.

Coming to the realization that she was on the wrong career path was not easy for Lynnette. It took a year of psychotherapy to treat the resulting depression and feelings of failure. It took another year of self-discovery and career exploration to discover new career goals. Eventually, Lynnette left the doctoral program to become a curator at a science museum.

Many community college students make career mistakes similar to Lynnette's—they forge ahead with a program of study without knowing whether or not they'll actually enjoy the career they're training for. If you don't take the time to research jobs that interest you and find out what they're really like on a day-to-day basis, then you may find yourself in a miserable job. You'd also have a bucket load of debt, so you'd have to keep the lousy job just to pay off your education (on the bright side, you'd keep my friends who are psychotherapists in business).

91 Underestimate the Consequences of Not Getting a Degree

I've a friend Jane who's said to me at least a thousand times, "I should've finished college." She says this whenever she was passed over for a promotion or she applied for a job where a degree was required. If anything, I think she should go back to college because she feels like she left something unfinished. I imagine that it's like those times when I've left a project half-finished; and can't function until I finish it (this rarely happens, so don't go diagnosing me with OCD!). Jane left college unfinished because she wasn't ready for it when she started.

If you're not ready for college—maybe you're a student who's only in college to keep your car insurance or to make your parents happy—then you're wasting both your time and mine. If you aren't ready for school, be honest with yourself and your parents. Maybe you need to tour the world, or work at a job you'd enjoy. You can always go back to school in a few years when you're more mature. There's really no point in going to college unless you're willing to put enough into your studies to get something out.

If you don't get a degree, you will likely make significantly less money than your peers who do. If you're happy with your life, maybe this won't be so bad. However, if you're one of those people who'll always feel like you left something unfinished and as a result have regrets, then you need to finish your degree.

92 Overestimate the Consequences of Getting a Degree

Davis and I were chatting after class.

"Dude, I can't wait until I get my BA degree and start making bank!"

"What do you want to do after college?"

"I don't know yet, I just know I'm going to make a lot of money."

"Who's going to pay you all this money?"

"Dude, if I had a degree, people would be lined up to give me a good job!"

"You're lucky, because most people, even college graduates, have to beg for a job."

"No way, if you get a degree, then you've got it made."

"When you get your diploma, there won't be any employers waiting there with job offers."

"Yeah, but I can just go apply for a great job and it's mine."

I gave up.

I've encountered many students who, like Davis, have unrealistic expectations about life after college graduation. These students don't realize that a college degree is the *minimum* qualification needed to apply for most *entry-level* positions.

It may take you ten to fifteen years after college graduation to reach a lifestyle that approximates the one you imagine falling into your lap as soon as you receive a baccalaureate. In fact, the entire first year after I received my *doctorate,* I only made eight-thousand dollars. It's a lot of work climbing the career ladder, so be prepared for a humbling experience.

STRATEGIES FOR SUCCESSFUL STUDENTS

- Map out your plan of study for the next two to four years
- Read the *College Catalog*
- Write out your short- and long-term goals
- Identify your skills, values, and interests
- Start career research now
- Develop realistic expectations for your future

EXERCISE 8.1 *Goals*

This worksheet is designed to help you identify your current and future goals.

GOAL	CURRENT	5 YEARS	10 YEARS
Health, physical			
Relationship, social, family			
Creative, artistic			
Economic, financial, career			
Intellectual, educational			
Spiritual, intra-personal, emotional			

Once you have completed filling in your goals, go back and ask yourself:

1. Which goal is the most important to you today?

2. How do your *educational* goals rate in comparison to your other goals?

EXERCISE 8.2 *Career Planning Self-Assessment*

This exercise is designed to help you take the first step in planning your career.

Skills
List 10 adjectives that describe your personality.

What are your strengths? Weaknesses?

List skills you possess that can be used in any occupation (e.g., writing, listening, operating equipment, computing, interacting with others).

Interests
In your free time, what activities do you enjoy doing?

Do you prefer to work with people, information, or things?

Values
If you were responsible for giving away a million dollars to a charity, which one(s) would you give the money to? Why?

What social or world issues are most important to you?

What sort of lifestyle do you want (e.g., predictable schedule, frequent travel)?

EXERCISE 8.3   Reflection

Please use the following space to reflect on what you've learned from this chapter, and how it can be applied to your life.

Personal and College Resources

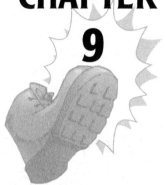

Loneliness: if you find yourself struggling with loneliness, you're not alone. And yet you are alone. So very alone.

—www.despair.com

Many people want you to succeed in college. Of course, your parents want you to succeed (it gives them bragging rights with their friends and acquaintances). For instance, I have been shopping with my mom and she's made a point of telling the sales clerk that I have a doctorate. The clerk could care less, but hell, her daughter has a doctorate so she'll work it into the conversation somehow. Your parents would love to brag about you, too.

Your professors want you to succeed as well. They are contributing directly to your success (by teaching you), but they also contribute indirectly by serving on committees focused on such topics as student learning and retention, participating in professional organizations such as "Teaching of Psychology," and attending national conferences with titles like "Best Practices in Undergraduate Education." The most dedicated faculty spend a significant portion of their lives dedicated to your success.

However, there are many other less visible people who also want you to succeed: counselors, librarians, department chairs, administrators, tutors, peer counselors, student government and activities leaders, campus psychologists, elected board members, health practitioners, publishing houses, online tutoring services, and many more.

No matter what your challenge, there is a professional to assist you in meeting it:

- *Counselors* help you make choices among the wide range of courses and programs that are available at your college and prepare you to transfer to a four-year institution or apply to a graduate program.
- *Extended Opportunity Programs and Services (EOPS)* coordinators assist educationally- or financially-challenged students.
- *Disabled Student Services* professionals provide testing and assistance for students with learning or other disabilities.
- *Financial Aid* counselors help you find money for college.
- *Campus Psychologists* help students whose studies are hampered by personal or emotional problems.
- *Child Care Centers* watch over your children so you can attend classes.

These are merely examples; your college catalog or Web site provides a more extensive list of available services at your college. With all of these resources, there is virtually no reason to flunk out of college. So many resources exist, that if you flunk out of college, *it's your own fault*. Still, if you're determined, this chapter can show you how to fail in spite of all these resources.

93 Allow Your Parents to Intervene on Your Behalf

One day, during office hours, I answered the phone.

"Hi, is this Dr. Cannon?" a voice asked.

"Yes, this is she."

"Hi, I'm calling because my son Carl is in one of your classes and he is concerned about his grade."

"Uh, huh [rolls eyes]. So why isn't Carl talking to me?" I ask, hoping that he has just had his tonsils out and that explains why his *mommy* is calling.

"Well, he is a little uncomfortable talking to you, because he is a responsible young man, and yet he seems to be doing so poorly in your course."

Did she just say *responsible*? This is his mommy calling, right? So I ask, "Just out of curiosity, how old is Carl?"

"Nineteen," she says.

"Well, I can't legally talk about an adult student's grades with anybody other than the student. In addition, I'm just plain uncomfortable with the idea that a nineteen-year-old, so-called-responsible-adult's mother is calling instead of him."

Now mom asks, "Are you being smart with me?"

"No, I'm just refusing to speak with you regarding your son. He needs to come in and see me in person. Tell him I promise not to bite him. If he chooses to speak to you about his grades later on, that's his business—but I won't discuss his grades with you."

Hmm, part of me thinks I should give this woman *my* mom's phone number so the two of them could duke it out. (Nah, my mom's a pit bull—she'd have this lady

ryanwinn.com

for lunch!) I wonder, if you aren't mature enough to speak to your professor yourself, are you really ready for college? When you finish college, or even an advanced degree, are you going to have your mommy call the CEO of your company and make him or her explain to her why you didn't get the promotion you thought you deserved?

At some point, parents need to let go of their children. College is that time. You'll get much more respect if you handle your own concerns.

94 Use Parents as Piggy Banks

Imagine running across the following job description in your local newspaper.

> Wanted: Young adult. Will pay all your expenses including car payment, insurance, gas, clothes, food, rent, utilities, college expenses, plus spending money. Medical and dental benefits included. Duties include doing absolutely nothing as long as you enroll in college classes. You need not complete or even attend classes as long as you enroll and at least pretend to attend.

Does this sound too good to be true? This is the deal that many students seem to make with their parents, who are happy to financially support their adult children as long as they look like they are attending college.

If I were financing a child's education, I would demand to see his transcripts at the end of the semester (to verify that he actually made significant progress toward a degree). And after one semester of insufficient progress, I'd throw his worthless keister out on the street. Sound harsh? That is exactly what would happen to any non-working, parentless adult in our society.

I have even seen students go as far as to threaten to leave home so their parents will buy their loyalty; their parents, in an attempt to avoid empty-nest syndrome, will pay them any amount to keep them living at home. In my course, Mandy mentioned that her parents promised to pay for her education plus give her a car and an expense account if she stayed at home for her college years. My jaw dropped.

"You're joking, right? They are *paying you* to live with them?"

"Yeah."

I was born when my sisters were twelve and sixteen years old, which means that by the time I moved off to college my parents had been parenting for over thirty-five years. I suspect they did a little, "We're done, we're free!" celebration dance when I left (at least that's what I'd do). Who in their right mind wants their adult children around badly enough to pay them to stay (and do nothing)?

Now if Mandy were a straight A student doing volunteer work to save homeless children and serving as president of the student government association, with no time to work a real job, then I'd be all in support of her parents helping her out. In fact, I'm more often shocked to see exceptional students struggling because their affluent parents are unwilling to help them at all, forcing them to reduce their academic load and increase hours at their part-time (or full-time) jobs. However, Mandy was getting a D in my class, rarely attended, and was immature and arrogant when she did attend (she frequently made derogatory comments about how stupid and unsuspecting her parents were to give her money).

One day in class, I shocked Mandy by telling her I'd fantasized about calling her parents and telling them to kick her out of the house. I'd love to see her try to make it on her own in Orange County, California, where a dilapidated studio apartment in a crime-infested neighborhood rents for nine-hundred bucks a month. I suppose she could always share an apartment with Spike, the tattoo artist, who could double as a bodyguard in case any serious action went down in the neighborhood. Of course, she'd have to work full-time to earn the money for the apartment, which would take at least forty hours of work per week earning six dollars an hour. But if she rode the bus and didn't eat, she'd get by.

My point is this: be honest with your parents and yourself. If you aren't ready to attend college, aren't sure what to do with your life, and you don't want to work, fine—*tell that to your parents*. If your parents force you to go to college against your will, you will fail, your teachers will become burnt out, and your parents will eventually become angry. No one wins in that situation. Instead, find something you would like to do and go back to college if and when you're ready.

95 Spend Lots of Money So You Have to Work Long Hours

Jeanette was a bright twenty-one-year-old freshman working to support herself while attending college. She had a small apartment and a roommate, so she could've worked a reasonable number of hours and taken a comfortable twelve-unit load. However, Jeanette spent too much money. She bought clothes, makeup, CDs, DVDs, a stereo—even a new car. She went to the movies, to concerts, and on weekend getaways. She had to work full time to pay off everything she'd bought. By the end of the day, Jeannette was often too exhausted to endure a three-hour night class, so she skipped classes. Even on her nights off, she could barely stay awake to complete her studies. Jeannette ended up missing so many classes that she fell behind, dropped half of her classes, and did poorly in the rest.

I meet at least five "Jeanettes" every semester. They could've afforded to attend college if they budgeted, but instead they went into debt and had to work their way out, with the effect of postponing their education.

College or graduate school may be the first time in your life you have to live on a restrictive budget. I'll be the first to admit that in college, I was a spoiled brat. Mom and Dad paid for everything from tuition, rent, and utilities to designer clothes, a gold watch, restaurant dining, and more. I guess, in a sense, you could say that I *was* employed: I probably "earned" fifty-thousand a year just being "daddy's little girl."

However, when I graduated from college, my parents cut me off. "Now that you're an adult, and a college graduate, you can support yourself."

I was stunned. "Huh? But, I want to go to graduate school! Aren't you going to help me?" I whined.

"No, our job is done."

"Omigod!"

Though I had a bachelor's degree, in my first year as a graduate student I made just twelve-thousand per year working as a teaching assistant. I was being paid for twenty hours a week, but like all the other TAs I was actually working as many as eighty hours per week (you do the math—there are third world countries that pay a higher wage).

For the first time in my life, I had to learn to budget. If I couldn't afford something, I didn't buy it. I didn't put more on my credit cards than I could pay off at the end of the month. I got by because I never bought anything that wasn't completely necessary to survive.

As a former Southern California "mall babe," I suffered terribly. I bought clothing at secondhand stores. My husband and I together subsisted on fifty dollars worth of food per week, mostly by making a crockpot meal of beans each week and eating it for lunch and dinner every day. I did, however, purchase anything and everything I needed for my studies: books, a copy card account, paper, and a computer.

Was it worth it? Would I do it all again? You bet! I now earn a comfortable living and can buy whatever I want (within reason).

The trick to money management is to manage your money well enough to stay in college and take the maximum number of units possible for your situation.

96 Say, "I Can't Afford the Textbook"

Rick couldn't afford to buy the textbook, so he asked me to place a copy of it on reserve at the college library. I'm always happy to do this if I can; however, I did notice that Rick was wearing $150 shoes, so I found his request a bit odd. The same was true for Cynthia and her $300 purse. Or Deb, whose boobs (which are impossibly high and never move) must have cost at least $5,000.

It's amazing how many students claim to suffer financial hardship while they are wearing designer jeans, sporting salon hairstyles, and exhibiting expensive manicures. A few of these students have even admitted to me that they already spent the money mom or dad gave them for books on something else. For anyone who blows their textbook money on other purchases, I have one word: *priorities*.

For those of you who struggle financially, textbooks are likely to be your biggest educational expense. If you really can't afford to purchase your textbooks, there are plenty of options:

- Ask the teacher to place a copy on reserve at the library for you if possible
- Buy a used book
- Use an older edition (ask your professor if this will be acceptable)
- Borrow one from a classmate (please remember to return it promptly)
- Check with your college for sources of financial aid specifically geared toward textbook purchases for needy students
- Sell something you don't need (eBay?) to raise the needed funds
- Get a temporary part-time job (maybe the college bookstore needs extra help at the start of the semester, this sometimes includes an employee discount, check at your college)

However, don't use a lack of funds as an excuse to avoid reading or completing assignments. Quite a few students wait until the third week of the semester and then apologize for failing to do an assignment. Saying, "I meant to start the reading, but I was waiting for my paycheck to purchase the book" doesn't cut it when there are forty-nine other students in the class who have one you could've borrowed for a day or two, as well as a copy freely available in the library.

97 Ignore Sources of Financial Aid

Last semester I received a frantic email from the scholarship office: there were several scholarships available, the due date for applying was rapidly approaching, and no one had applied for them. The email begged faculty to encourage worthy students to apply.

I mentioned to Franklin that there was a scholarship he should apply for and he replied, "I don't have time."

"What do you mean you 'don't have time'? You walk a few yards to the scholarship office, pick up an application, hand me the faculty recommendation form, and turn the whole thing in. It'll take thirty-minutes tops."

"No, it's a waste of time. Anyway, I might not get it."

"So far, no one else has even applied for it. I'd say the odds are great!"

"It's just too much work to fill out the application."

Let's do the math. The scholarship was worth about two-thousand dollars, so far there was zero competition for it, and filling out the application would take about half an hour. Franklin was turning down "work" that amounted to a pay rate of up to four-thousand dollars per hour. Who "doesn't have time" to earn four-thousand dollars an hour? The best part is that a major reason why Franklin "doesn't have time" is that, like many students, he works part-time—where he makes about ten bucks an hour.

There are many sources of financial aid for students. Not all of them require you to demonstrate financial need; some are based on merit. It's up to you to go to your financial aid office to discover where these sources are and how to apply for them.

What else can you do if you're really desperate for funds to pay for college?

- Work full-time in the summer or winter to pay off debts and save for the upcoming semester. This frees up spring and fall to focus on your courses.
- Look for ways to make money without really working. For instance, many people are willing to pay a responsible college student to watch their house while they are on vacation. Some families offer room and board in exchange for work.
- Check into the possibility of consolidating existing debts into low-cost student loans.
- Seek out sources of free money through state and federal grant programs.
- Sell stuff you don't use or could live without. For example, if you sold your car you could save the money you spend on car payments, repairs, gas, and insurance. Remind yourself that it's only temporary; in a few years, you'll graduate and treat yourself to a new car.

98 Avoid New Student Orientations

I enjoy the small, friendly atmosphere of our campus, which (assuming you're healthy) can be traveled from one end to the other in about five minutes. If someone took a bit of time stopping and describing where all the campus services (e.g., admissions and records, counseling) were located, a tour might stretch to fifteen minutes. With such an intimate size, it's somewhat surprising to me that many of my students have no idea where anything is located on our campus.

After a fifteen-minute class break, Donnie returned in a state of agitation. She complained, "The campus bookstore was out of the vegetarian sandwiches I like. I'm so mad! I didn't eat anything for lunch and I'm starving."

"So why didn't you go to the cafeteria and get one? They have a larger selection, anyway."

"What cafeteria?"

"It's in the building right next to the bookstore. It's about a two-minute walk from the bookstore."

"I've been going here for two years, and I didn't even know we *had* a cafeteria!"

Like Donnie, many students are unaware of the location of many campus resources: the library, tutoring center, computer center, financial aid office, and so on. A simple self-guided tour around campus during your first week on campus is not a bad idea. A "virtual" tour of the college Web site is also a must.

A guided tour is even better. Most colleges arrange orientation tours for new students: campus resources are explained and the location of available services pointed out, saving you the time and effort of figuring this stuff out for yourself.

I may owe my academic life to the counselor who led my first college orientation. She said something that forever changed my perspective on college life: "You start college with a clean slate. If you get enough transferable units, then your high school record (mine was bad) will never be looked at by anyone again. It's as if you begin with a 4.0 GPA, and only you can destroy that perfect record."

It was a second chance. Good thing I took it, too, because after you've bombed high school, a community college is your only gateway to a baccalaureate degree.

99 Avoid the People Who Can Help You Succeed

Bill whined, "I don't understand this 'arranged hour' that we are supposed to do."

"It's simple. To get credit in the class, you have to spend one hour a week doing an assignment outside of class. You get to choose: either do some online activities, or go over to the tutoring center and work with a tutor for an hour."

"Wow, that sucks because I don't have a computer at home."

"I guess that means you choose the tutoring option."

"I don't want tutoring. That is *so* lame."

"You got a 59% on the first exam. *That's* lame."

"I know. That was my fault for not studying. I'm going to study from now on."

"A tutor can help you study; they can quiz you or review the material that is difficult for you."

"I guess."

Tutoring is just one of several options for an assignment in one of my courses. It's an option that very few students choose to do. I suspect, from the way my students cringe when I mention it, that many students are embarrassed about seeking tutoring; they feel that it's a sign of academic weakness to need help studying. Funny, they don't seem quite so embarrassed to fail my classes.

If you're really determined to fail in college, make sure you avoid all the other places that contain people who care whether or not you succeed: the library, the writing center, the computer center, and the health center. For instance, many students never visit the library even though there is an invaluable and underused resource there to help students with their homework—*reference librarians.* Yes, librarians do a lot more than swipe your ID card when you check out books. They help you locate and obtain materials for reports, explain how to use search tools to select appropriate resources, and even offer free workshops on how to conduct research and use the library's resources. But if you'd rather flounder on your own, by all means, do.

100 Stay Away from Free Services

Summer had been in one of my classes before; I remembered her as a lively and engaging student. However, this semester she seemed increasingly gloomy, so I shouldn't have been surprised when she came to see me before class and asked if it was normal to stay up all night crying. I walked Summer to our campus's clinical psychologist's office, where she met with a therapist and made arrangements to follow up two days later.

Summer never made the follow-up appointment. She confessed to me that she felt stupid because she'd overreacted and that she didn't think she needed psychotherapy. Nevertheless, what would've been the harm in having a few additional sessions with a psychotherapist? The service was *free;* where else can you get free therapy? Summer could've benefited from discussing the situation that led her to speak to me in the first place, and maybe learned techniques to recognize and counter stress before it reached astronomic proportions.

Instead, Summer faded away that semester; she failed the class and I haven't seen her since. Apparently, she took time off to deal with her personal problems. Unfortunately, for Summer, if she keeps using ineffective coping strategies, she may end up needing psychotherapy in the "real world" where it will likely cost her well over one-hundred dollars an hour.

If you look at your college's catalog or Web site, then you will discover a variety of free or low-cost services offered to students: psychotherapy, health care, birth control, fitness centers, exercise classes, no-interest computer loans, and much more. These same services cost a great deal more if purchased off campus, so take advantage of them while you can.

101 Don't Be a "Joiner"

Far from flunking out of our college, Kim was a candidate for valedictorian. She really deserved the honor—her transcript read like a dream, she achieved a 4.0 GPA and she'd taken a rigorous series of courses in math and science. Her academic accomplishments were far more impressive than any of the other candidates; however, Kim was not chosen for the honor. Why? She hadn't engaged in *any* extracurricular or service-related activities.

was not chosen for the honor. Why? She hadn't engaged in *any* extracurricular or service-related activities.

It is important to be well-rounded; and to *be* well-rounded, you need to do something besides take classes—join a club or the debate team, run for a student government position, or volunteer for your favorite charity. Students who are actively involved in their college tend to persist in their studies more than students who attend classes and then simply go home. Get involved and people will learn your name, you'll feel as though you fit in, and you'll develop a social support network. Otherwise, it may be too easy to drop out—who'd even notice?

STRATEGIES FOR SUCCESSFUL STUDENTS

- Many people are rooting for your success; cultivate these supporters
- Cut the strings from your parents and be responsible for your own behavior
- Make a budget and stick to it; remind yourself that you're sacrificing the "extras" today for a brighter future
- Look for creative ways to squeeze money out of your budget and search for financial aid
- Become familiar with your college's resources and use them to the fullest
- Get involved in activities outside the classroom

EXERCISE 9.1   *Campus Resources*

This exercise will help you become familiar with the resources available to you at your college.

1. Where is the admissions office?

2. Where can I get information on planning my schedule and preparing for graduation or transfer?

3. Where can I find the *College Catalog* and the *Schedule of Classes*? If there is more than one place, list them all.

4. Where can I get health or psychological services? How much do these services cost?

5. What clubs might be of interest to me? How do I join a club?

6. Where do I get a student identification card?

7. When is the last day to drop a class?

8. When are books bought back?

9. Where is the financial aid office?

10. Where is the tutoring center?

11. Where is the computing center?

12. Where is the library?

13. Where do students with disabilities go for assistance?

14. When do I register for next semester?

15. What sports teams does our school have?

16. Can I go on tours of universities? Who arranges these tours?

17. Where can I get information on career planning?

Name: _____   Date: _____

EXERCISE 9.2   Financial Resources: Monthly Budget Worksheet

Monthly Income

Source	Budgeted amount (A)	Actual amount received (B)	Difference (A–B)
Job			
Parents			
Loans			
Scholarships			
Financial aid			
Other			
Subtotal			

Monthly Expenses

Source	Budgeted amount (C)	Actual amount spent (D)	Difference (C–D)
Housing			
Utilities			
Food			
Transportation			
Phone			
Insurance			
School expenses			
Fun			
Other			
Subtotal			

Total Savings at Month's End

Subtotal Income – Subtotal Expenses = _____ (I sure hope this is a positive number!)

Identify 3 ways to earn additional money.

Identify 3 ways to save money (by trimming expenses).

EXERCISE 9.3 Reflection

Please use the following space to reflect on what you've learned from this chapter, and how it can be applied to your life.

Apply It

For each of the scenarios below identify which of the 101 strategies from the previous chapters was used by each student. Hint: there are likely to be several strategies for each scenario. Discuss your answer in the space provided.

102 *Alex*

"Dr. Cannon, I think I forgot to sign in on the roll sheet last Thursday. Can you check?"

"If you only forgot one time, it won't make a difference. Just don't forget again."

"I might have forgotten to sign it the last three weeks."

"Three weeks?!"

"It's not my fault because it never made it around to my seat."

"Alex, you come in late quite frequently and that must be why you missed the sign in sheet. If you come in late, it is your responsibility to come up after class to sign in."

"I was here, so I think I should get credit for being here."

"As it says in the syllabus, you are responsible for showing up on time *and* signing in."

About two weeks later, she comes up after class and says, "I was here Tuesday; I just forgot to sign in."

"Alex, I've explained the attendance policy to you a couple of times."

We repeated the same conversation two more times that semester.

The following spring semester, Alex was back in one of my classes. The second week of the term, she asked, "Am I going to lose points because I forgot to sign in last week?"

103 *Piper*

It is summer session and my online Introduction to Child Psychology course is in its second of four weeks. The class is really 16 weeks crammed into four. Students read 3 heavy-duty chapters per week, take 3 quizzes, and complete 3 discussion boards. Honestly, it's tough.

When Piper emailed me begging to add the course, I was stunned. The course is nearly half over. Would she ask to join a fall class at midterms? She'd have to take zeroes on the first three quizzes and the first three discussion boards because I don't allow late work or makeups. She would need to read 6 chapters that week. The midterm was two days away. There is no way she could succeed unless she is already a child psychologist!

I know how intense short courses are because I once made a bad decision to take an online four-week Real Estate class during summer session at another college. I had no background in real estate or even business courses for that matter, but I had just started investing in property and wanted to know more. Reading 3 chapters per week made me want to cry. All I did for that month was read and study. It wouldn't have been as bad had I taken Jungian Psychology—not my area of expertise, but at least I have some background knowledge. I knew the class would be challenging, and had I missed the first week I'd have waited for the following term.

I wondered how a student could think that joining an accelerated class that is half-over would be no big deal. Did she expect me to allow late work, to accommodate her in other ways, or would she want to take the final early so she could fly to Tahiti? This was a real head scratcher for me.

The very same day that I pondered Piper's email, I happened to read an article entitled, "Is Gen Z #Unemployable?" by Dan Merritts who stated that,

> "The students of Generation Z are a confident group that almost always believe they are ready to take the next step or take on the next task, no matter how prepared they actually are. Whether it's taking a final exam after one night's worth of cramming or earning a promotion in their first year, today's youth truly believe they can get the job done."

It appeared that Piper was either overconfident or she expected me to accommodate her.

104 Joe

I'm watching the tryouts for the TV show, "So You Think You Can Dance". It reminds me a lot of college: young adults dreaming of success and hoping to reach the top of their profession, expert judges providing guidance and feedback.

But what if the show was even more like college?

Nigel: "How long have you been dancing (studying)?"

Contestant: "I just started last night. But I was up all night practicing."

Nigel: "You just weren't good enough compared to some of our other contestants. You have no musicality and you tripped twice."

Contestant: "But I really, really WANT this! I want it so bad!"

Nigel: "Why didn't you say so? Come and get a ticket to Las Vegas! I mean, you *showed up* and you *tried*. That's the most important thing."

Right.

Most of my spring semester's Introduction to Psychology class included students who started studying for their exam the night before and yet expected to get an A on it.

Take Joe Student, for example. Joe showed up to class virtually every day. However, he missed all but one quiz in the course. The quizzes are online, and can be taken twice. That means, you could take a quiz once, bomb it, look up all the answers, and still get a 10/10. There is no reason not to get 10 points every week. Joe was a bright student. He got a C in the class.

Last Name	First Name	Syllabus Quiz	Ch01_Quiz	Ch02_Quiz	Ch03_Quiz	Ch04_Quiz	Ch05_Quiz	Ch06_Quiz	Ch07_Quiz	Ch12_Quiz	Ch13_Quiz	Ch15_Quiz	Ch17_Quiz	Exam01	Exam02	Exam03	Exam04	Participation	*TOTAL	GRADE
Points Possible		25	10	10	10	10	10	10	10	10	10	10	10	100	100	100	100	25	550	
Student	Joe	0	0	0	7	0	0	0	0	0	0	0	0	88	74	63	73	25	330	C
Better Student	Joe	25	10	10	10	10	10	10	10	10	10	10	10	88	74	63	73	25	458	B
Even Better Student	Joe	25	10	10	10	10	10	10	10	10	10	10	10	92	78	68	76	25	474	A

Imagine if Joe became Joe Better Student and took every single quiz that semester. Let's suppose that is his only improvement: he still didn't take the optional Exam 5 to improve his lowest exam score. If he just simply spent an extra ½ hour each week to do the quizzes, he'd have earned a B in the class.

Taking the quizzes has an additional benefit, in that some of the questions are similar or even identical to the exam questions. If Joe had taken all of the quizzes, I suspect that his exam scores would have been higher, as seen in Joe Even Better Student's scores.

A successful dancer practices more than 8 hours per day. The average college student spends less than two hours studying per day[1]. I'm not surprised that many students leave college no more knowledgeable and in comparison to their peers[2]. Sad yes, surprised no.

105 Lorna

I had just received a new "friend" request in my Facebook account. Lorna was a student in two of my advanced psychology courses 2 or 3 years ago.

"How nice," I thought, "she's thinking of me and wants to reconnect."

I'm Facebook friends with former students whom I've gotten to know relatively well. Usually these are psychology majors, like Lorna who have taken several classes with me and done well. Fair warning: I post a nauseating number of dog photos. Just saying.

About three days after I accepted her friend request, Lorna sends a private message saying, "I don't know if you remember me, but I took a few classes with you, blah, blah, blah."

Of course I remember her, I only have 100 some odd Facebook friends because I only accept requests from people I know (the one time I accepted a request from someone I didn't personally know he turned out to be a creeper).

Lorna's message goes on to ask me for a letter of recommendation for graduate school.

I unfriended her.

If Lorna *only* wanted a letter of recommendation, she should have emailed my professional email account. Her timing was so awkward—she "friend" requested me, asked me if I knew who she was, and then immediately asks for a recommendation letter? She could have "friend" requested me two years ago, liked a few dog pictures over the years (not even the ones where one of my dogs just looked cute, but one where we won something big at a dog show), or she could have wished me a happy birthday once a year. Made it less obvious that she wanted something.

Facebook is not for professional relationships; for that, there are other tools like Linked In. I'm friends with former students on Facebook, so I know when they graduate, get married, have babies, and so forth. I laugh at some of their posts and cry at others. They like my occasional, "Today something funny happened in class" stories. If after 3 years of this they ask me for a letter via private message, it doesn't make me feel used.

Had I written a letter for Lorna, I suspect that I'd never hear from her again until she needed a letter of recommendation for more graduate school or for a job. And then again when she wanted one for a promotion.

106 Nicky

"My sister Nicky had your class two years ago."

"I remember Nicky, she was in 2 or 3 of my classes. How is she doing now?"

"She transferred to the UC and I guess she's doing really well because she is on the Dean's list," Stella said.

"That's nice, but I thought I heard some hesitation before you answered."

"I really don't know how she made the Dean's list. She never studies and she rarely goes to class. I study super hard and barely get B's."

I suspected that Stella, who ended up earning an A in my class, would be the more successful of the two sisters. Stella works harder, and is more engaged during and after class than Nicky ever was. Nicky had the great misfortune of being very bright. So bright that she didn't put in much effort. She just breezed through her classes, got her A's and went home.

"The only thing I worry about is that Nicky isn't doing any of the things that will get her a job, or into a graduate program."

"What do you mean, Dr. Cannon?"

"She isn't very involved in college and so she'll leave without getting the most important thing she needs—three really great letters of recommendation from faculty."

If Nicky asked me for a letter it would be super short.

> Dear Admissions Committee:
> Nicky got an A in two of my classes.
> Please accept her into your program.
> Sincerely,
> Dr. Cari Cannon

When you compare that to the longer, more glowing letters that I've written, usually about extensive work done by students in the Psychology Honor Society—raising funds, conducting independent research, volunteering—Nicky doesn't stand a chance. The most frequently assigned grade in many colleges today is an A[3]. Everyone is getting A's. Compared to students who've done extensive work outside of the classroom, getting an A isn't enough to stand out.

107 Red

"I tried to submit my paper in Blackboard, but I got an error message saying that my paper couldn't be submitted since it was past the deadline, but it wasn't past the deadline. It was 11:59 pm."

"You're joking, right? You waited until the absolute last minute! When I said the paper was due at 11:59 pm that means that at 12:00 am it's late, so I don't know what to tell you."

"But it wasn't late. It was still 11:59 pm."

"Luckily, the first paper is worth very few points, so it won't devastate your grade. Make sure to get the next couple papers in on time because they are worth progressively more. And if you are having problems, get them addressed several days before the paper is due, so I have time to help you."

Red whined in my office for over an hour. By the time she finally left, she had used up all my good will for her lifetime. She didn't get her paper in on time, and she earned a zero, just as the syllabus promised. Not taking no for an answer was her first mistake.

"Dr. Cannon, Blackboard refused my final paper and it was on time! I took a picture of the clock on my computer to prove it! It was 11:58 pm!"

"Not again!" Her clock must be slow. "I can't believe you didn't learn your lesson last time! Why did you wait until the last minute? If you had trouble submitting the paper at noon, then I could've helped you figure it out. But when you plan to login and submit your paper at 11:55 pm, you are really begging for disaster!"

Red could not be mollified. She cried, she whined, and she pleaded. I told her to go to the help desk and have them offer proof that she submitted her paper on time. Instead, she went to the dean. The dean asked the help desk for the time stamp on the computer. According to the help desk, she attempted to submit her paper at 12:04 am.

A few days later, Red came to my office with a woman in her 40s who claimed to be her mother's friend. She was a "witness" claimed Red. She saw her working on her paper and saw the time stamp on the computer when Red tried to submit it.

"I'm sorry, but I can't discuss an adult student's work with anyone other than the student."

"The student is right there! TALK TO HER!" she screamed.

Is this nut for real?

"I'm going to have to ask you to leave my office."

"NO!"

Did this person think she was helping Red? My syllabus explicitly states, "The instructor will not discuss your grade and/or standing in the course with parents, friends, relatives etc. If you are under age 18 and this will pose a problem for you or your parents, then please do not take this course."

Today's students believe that if they are doing poorly in a class, that the instructor has to help find ways to raise their grade. This might have been true in high school, but it is neither required nor expected of college professors. In truth we are more than happy to answer questions about course content or assignments before they are due, but once the assignment has been missed, or poorly done, you receive the grade you deserve. End of story.

108 Larry

"Dr. Cannon, can you proof read my paper for my Advanced Experimental Psychology class?"

Larry, a former student of mine, is now a student at UC Santa Cruz. It is pretty nervy of him to ask me to proof-read his paper. But I remember that I've got a list of 3-4 articles that I needed to download from a University library because my own college library doesn't have the journals. I see a trade.

"Okay, I'll give it a light proofreading, if you can download a couple articles and send them to me."

"Thanks, Dr. Cannon, you're the best!"

I did the proofreading that night and returned the paper with some corrections.

I never received the articles. A few days later, I reminded him. "I'll get them tonight," he said.

He never did.

A week later I asked another former student to do me a favor and get them. She did. Literally within 5 minutes of me asking. She also goes to UCSC. Hmmm. I don't think they were difficult to get.

I'll bet anyone reading this that Larry asks me to write him a recommendation letter for graduate school next year. The problem is he is a consistent flake. He gets A's in all his classes, but he can't be bothered to do anything else.

Larry was the Treasurer of our Psychology Club. He was supposed to get the account balance. He didn't. He was supposed to show up to the officer's meeting. He didn't. He was supposed to locate a guest speaker for the next meeting. Didn't do that either. You could count on *not* counting on Larry.

I remember my first few days in graduate school. I was told that classes no longer mattered. "Every student here got A's in all their undergraduate classes and we expect you to maintain your grades, but most of your time and effort should be spent on conducting research," said my graduate advisor.

The most important job of a graduate student is the work done outside the classroom in addition to course work. I finally understood why it was so important that I worked as a Behavior Therapist in the UCLA Autism Clinic as an undergraduate. Here's my letter for Larry:

Dear Graduate Admissions Committee:

Larry got A's in all his classes and held the title Treasurer of the Psychology Club.

Sincerely,

Cari B. Cannon, Ph.D.

Footnotes

1. For example see:

   http://nsse.indiana.edu/NSSE_2013_Results/pdf/NSSE_2013_Annual_Results.pdf

   And

   http://www.collegeparents.org/members/resources/articles/your-college-student-investing-enough-time-studying

2. Arum, R. (2011). *Academically Adrift: Limited Learning on College Campuses.* University of Chicago Press.

3. For example see:

   http://www.bostonmagazine.com/news/blog/2013/12/04/frequently-assigned-grade-harvard/

INDEX

CPSIA information can be obtained at www.ICGtesting.com
Printed in the USA
LVOW02s1810180815

449944LV00004B/4/P